THE ADVENTURES OF GAMRIE TICKLE

THE ADVENTURES OF

GAMRIE TICKLE

Aletheia Short Stories

E M WILKIE

RITCHIE
John Ritchie Publishing

40 Beansburn, Kilmarnock, Scotland

THE ADVENTURES OF GAMRIE TICKLE
E M WILKIE

Copyright © 2018 by John Ritchie Ltd.
40 Beansburn, Kilmarnock, Scotland

www.ritchiechristianmedia.co.uk

ISBN-13: 978 1 912522 23 1

Written by E M Wilkie
Illustrated by E M Wilkie
www.aletheiabooks.co
Copyright © 2018

Unless otherwise indicated, Scripture quotations are taken from:
The Holy Bible, New King James Version®.
© 1982 by Thomas Nelson, Inc. Used by permission. All rights reserved.
Printed and bound in Great Britain by Bell and Bain Ltd, Glasgow.

This book is also available as an ebook and audio book, and Bible Study Worksheets are also available. For more information, please visit
https://www.aletheiabooks.co/

CONTENTS

INTRODUCTION

You should read this bit first!

This book contains a collection of stories about someone called Gamrie Tiberius Tickle. He lives in Aletheia – the city of Bible Truth located in the middle of the land of Err. Err is a dangerous place. It is utterly opposed to Aletheia. The people of Err want to change, assault, and even destroy the city of Bible Truth at its centre. They want everyone to think the way that they do – in fact, you can believe anything you want as long as you *don't* believe that there is only one version of Truth, and that it is found in the Bible. So the people of Aletheia, who trust in the Bible, must learn to defend and fight for the Truth. Gamrie Tiberius Tickle is one of them.

In case you've never been there, I should explain that being in the land of Err isn't like living in ordinary places in the UK or the USA or in other countries of our world. You see, the land of Err is *another world entirely* and things that happen there could *never* happen where you or I live. Objects that are symbols or illustrations or examples of something where we live *actually come to life* in Err. So, for example, when the Bible talks about how wrong things can snare us and cause us to sin, in the land of Err Snares become real, frightening creatures. I'm sure you'll get the idea of how things work in Err as we go along.

These stories are about some things that happened to Gamrie Tickle as he grew up in Aletheia. Quite often, they're about the things that went wrong! If you've read *The Broken Journey* (Aletheia Adventure Series Book 3), you will have met Gamrie Tickle before, in a dangerous adventure when he is an old man. In these stories he's much younger. In fact, our account starts about fifty years before the Aletheia Adventure Series. But Gamrie is just one of those people to whom interesting, exciting things always happen. If there's a fantastic adventure, terrible mishap, or deadly danger lurking around the corner, you can be sure Gamrie Tickle will walk right into it. So we will follow close behind him and watch what he does. But be on your guard! Unexpected things might happen…

P.S. Watch out for all the characters you might remember from the Aletheia Adventure Series!

1. THE BOOT CLEANER

Ever since he could remember, Gamrie Tiberius Tickle wanted to be a Rescuer of Aletheia. When he was young, his bedroom window overlooked the turrets and battlements of the high walls surrounding the mighty fortress of the Academy of Soldiers-of-the-Cross. This was where the Rescuers were based. From his window, Gamrie could see them on guard. Smart, stately ranks of Rescuers – primed and ready, alert for any danger, keeping watch from the highest towers of the fortress over the far reaches of the perilous land of Err. Uniformed men and women came and went through the massive castle doors. Gamrie liked to imagine the fights they had been in and all the fantastic, dangerous things they had seen.

Had they felt the chill of a scary, vaporous Snare? Their cobweb-like fingers could entangle you and carry you captive wherever they thought you should go.

Had a Stumble enmeshed their feet with its sticky octopus-like tendrils? Anyone who was unprepared could be tripped into their gluey hold and trapped for days.

What about a Sloth? They might look like harmless clouds, but they could send you to sleep with two blinks of their ve-ry slo-o-owly clo-s-ing e-e-ey-y-y-e-s.

As for Meddlers, personally Gamrie would like to capture one. A

Meddler would make a very angry pet, but he had a longing to tame one of these wicked, flying imps.

What about Gluttons? Gamrie wished one was able to cross the impenetrable boundary of the Water of Sound Doctrine into Aletheia. How he would love to see it at work! What it would be to watch one of these gnome-like creatures going about its business, adding shine and glamour to plain objects, deceiving and teasing and tempting people to give way to greed!

There were many other creatures, and there were also inventions – such as robotic Vanitors – living in the land of Err. Gamrie had once seen a picture of a Vanitor. He would love to have one to command and boss around.

In Gamrie's frequent daydreams that depicted farfetched adventures, none of these creatures were a problem to him. You see, like some Christians in our own land today, he didn't take these enemies of Bible Truth seriously. He dwelt on the glamour and heroism of Rescuers; not on the very real danger of these many clever, deceitful, treacherous adversaries. To him, the job of a heroic Rescuer was easy. One swipe of a fist and even the greatest creature went tumbling into the dust! The Rescuers were so great, so well-armed, so thoroughly trained for the fight, so unassailable. More than anything in the world, he wanted to be one of them. But, as these stories unfold, we will discover just how much Gamrie had to learn about the consequences, for himself and for those around him, of not being adequately prepared to guard against even the simplest enemy of Bible Truth.

About the armour of God

In his enthusiasm to be like the Rescuers, Gamrie tried to get as close to them as possible. At school, he had always been taught that a Christian must learn about the armour of God in order to be properly equipped to fight and defend against the creatures of Err. Since he must start somewhere in his quest to be a Rescuer, Gamrie decided to set up a boot-cleaning business by the front steps of the Academy of Soldiers-of-the-Cross. Not only would this get him close to the Rescuers, but it would also help him to learn about the boots of the armour of God.

He got up early before school and helped himself liberally to his mother's household supplies. Then he went to the Academy. Setting up his simple stall didn't take long. In a minute all was complete. He settled down to watch the Rescuers arrive for their duties.

For a very short time, Gamrie could have boasted that he was the only boot-cleaning service the Academy of Soldiers-of-the-Cross had ever had. But, to his astonishment, all the boots passing his stand were spotlessly clean! You see, experienced Rescuers did not dare to go about their business in less than fully-functioning, freshly-cleaned and carefully-prepared armour of God. It was no use taking about with you the dust and filth of Err. Every day was a new one in service as a Rescuer of the Academy of Soldiers-of-the-Cross. Every day you needed to put on fresh armour.

In case you don't know what I mean, I'll explain a bit about the armour of God. The Bible explains that a Christian should wear the armour of God. This isn't literal, real armour such as you might see in a museum or a stately home; not polished metal and gleaming swords. Actually, it's invisible and you put it on in your mind – by reading the Bible and praying. Of course, you need to prepare and put it on *every* day. In this way it's like dressing to fight in a daily battle, the way a Christian must do in order to fight temptations and defend the Truth of the Bible.

Because things are different in Aletheia, the armour is real and visible. Gamrie could see the Rescuers in their smart uniforms and armour; that's why he was going to offer to clean their armour boots.

The first customer

Although Gamrie could see the armour, he didn't know much about it. He prepared his stall and admired the gleaming armour boots passing by, wondering who else was engaged in the boot-cleaning business and how they managed to produce such incredibly shiny boots.

However, on day two of his venture, a young recruit rushed towards the front steps of the Academy. Even to Gamrie – who did not always notice obvious things – it was evident that the young man was late. The trainee was still flinging on his armour of God, fastening his belt of truth about him, and his boots weren't even tied! Laces were tangled and trailing and likely to trip him up at any moment. And the boots were definitely dirty and dusty from a previous mission.

"Young sir!" Gamrie called politely, waving one of the brushes he had 'borrowed' from his mother. "Clean your boots, sir!"

The young man rushed over. He stared down at the boy sitting cross-legged on the paving slabs. Now, Gamrie was a rather untidy boy with a thatch of thick brown hair that perpetually needed combing. The recruit noticed the wild hair, and the fact that the boy was waving about a long-handled brush that, strangely enough, looked like a *ladies' hair brush*. The boot-cleaner even had dirty shoes! He certainly wasn't a good advert for a boot-cleaning business, but the man couldn't afford to be fussy.

A bucket was standing there, containing cloudy water that had been liberally splashed over and around the boy and on the paving slabs. In addition, there were two glass jars – the size of jam jars – both containing a dark, unfamiliar substance. On one, a handwritten label, stuck over the top of something else, said, *'I think this is boot stuff'*. The other simply stated, *'Might come in handy'*.

Nothing about this curious boot-cleaning stand was reassuring. The young trainee definitely hesitated. All his basic training went against such an unknown fix for his ill-prepared attire. But desperation lent impulse to his need. "Just a quick brush up, to, umm, cover up the dirt a bit..." he said, ashamed at the state of his boots, although the boot-cleaner's shoes were definitely far worse. "Chief Wiseman is addressing us this morning, and I meant to get up early and have everything spotless, but…" He sighed deeply. He wasn't sure why he was confiding in this scruffy boy – who was probably running late for school and might also be in trouble himself.

"Chief Wiseman!" Gamrie was impressed and not in the least bit hurried. "Won't take long, sir," he promised. "If you like, I could tell you my best jokes while you wait."

"I really don't think…"

"What happens when you eat boot polish?" Already laughter was crinkling around the boy's bright blue eyes.

"I don't know…"

"You shine all the time!" Gamrie rocked back on his heels and laughed long and loudly and very merrily. "I made it up, you know," he said, wiping his eyes. "I thought up some good boot jokes when I got this job!"

Calling his impromptu stall with its 'borrowed' wares a *job* was such an exaggeration that it astonished the trainee. "I think I'd better go… I'm in a hurry, I'm afraid…" he stuttered, increasingly desperate to get away.

Gamrie immediately stuck the brush he held into the jar labelled *'I think this is boot stuff'*. Out came the brush with a generous quantity of thick black substance smeared all over it.

"Are you quite certain…?" The young man looked aghast as the hairbrush began to ooze dark liquid that proved to be not quite like solid boot polish after all. A drop splattered on the paving slab, and then another…

Down went the gooey brush firmly onto the trainee's armour

boots.

Gamrie began to rub the brush vigorously over both boots. "I think that... it just needs a good... rub... like this... and it will all come... bright and shinin'... I 'spect so... anyway..." His words were punctuated with the effort of smearing the black substance all over the boots, and even along the bottom of the young man's uniform.

Mesmerised, then horrified, the recruit stared at the sticky mess beneath which his boots were somewhere concealed. "What *is* that stuff?" he demanded.

Gamrie examined the side of the jar. "It says..."

"I can see what it says! I dare say *you* wrote the label!" cried the young man. "It says you only *think* that it's *boot stuff*, but what did you put into the jar?!"

"It's my first try," Gamrie said in an injured tone. "I can't be 'spected to get everythin' just right the first time, can I?"

The young man groaned. "It's not your fault," he said gloomily. "It's my own problem for not being prepared..."

Then, with fresh horror, he became aware of the man who had suddenly appeared beside them. Now he was in real trouble!

Lieutenant Reuben Duffle

The man who had quietly approached looked at the trainee and the boy with genuine astonishment and definite disapproval. He was a smart young man in the uniform of a lieutenant. He was young to be honoured with such a rank; evidently he was an exceptional Rescuer, and he was immediately recognised by both of them.

"Uh, Lieutenant Duffle, s-sir, sorry, sir, I'm running late, s-sir, b-but…"

"I'm cleanin' his boots, you see, sir," said the boy cheerfully. "I could do yours too, Lieutenant-sir, once I've finished these, but…" Gamrie studied the spotlessly shining boots worn by Lieutenant Reuben Duffle. He realised – with what was, for him, unusual perceptiveness – that his administrations would *not* be welcome.

"Were your boots dirty, Trainee… Dim View, is it?" asked Lieutenant Duffle, focussing on the recruit.

"Yes, sir. I had intended to get up early and prepare…"

"But you did not."

"No, sir," said the recruit sadly.

"Return to your lodgings and prepare your armour of God immediately," directed Lieutenant Duffle. "I don't like to imagine what this boy has been applying to your boots, but even if it takes the rest of the day you will clean and prepare yourself for your work and not leave your lodgings until you are properly shod. Understood?"

"Yes, sir, at once, sir," said the trainee. He attempted to hurry away, but this was made less dignified by the dreadful stickiness of his boots that now seemed congealed and stuck to the paving slabs outside the Academy.

At last, he freed himself – and fled.

The Lieutenant and Gamrie

Meanwhile, Gamrie extracted himself from the damp, sticky mess in which he had been seated and scrambled to his feet. Lieutenant Duffle bent down and poked a finger in the sticky substance on the paving slabs. "Treacle," he commented.

Gamrie's eyebrows shot up to his hairline. "Is it really?"

"What is your name, boy?"

"Gamrie Tickle, sir!" Gamrie saluted as he had practised so many times in his own room at home. It wasn't quite the effect he wanted, and it transferred treacle from his hand to his hair, but he was pleased to be able to practise on a real lieutenant.

Lieutenant Duffle reflected. "Hmm, Teffle and Trixie Tickle's son. I see. Shouldn't you be at school, Tickle?"

"Yes, sir, right away, sir, but you see…"

"I think, perhaps, you'd better go home first and change your clothes and tell your mother what you've been up to," said the lieutenant.

"Oh no, sir, I've been to school far worse than this, Lieutenant-sir…"

The lieutenant frowned. "This is not a matter for debate, Tickle. You *will* go home to your mother and you will never again attempt to clean boots here at the Academy." The lieutenant knew where the Tickles lived. He began to steer Gamrie in the direction of his home.

"I just thought I could help the Rescuers," Gamrie said glumly. "You see, I really want to be one…"

"Do you understand what makes a great Rescuer, Tickle?" asked the lieutenant.

"Being a Christian, sir," Gamrie said eagerly. "And I am a Christian, sir! Last summer I trusted in the Lord Jesus to take away my sins. Then I could see the armour of God, and I always wanted to be a Rescuer after that."

"It takes more than simply being a Christian to be an effective Rescuer, Tickle. Do you understand the importance of the armour of God?"

"It's important to help fight enemies in the land of Err," Gamrie replied promptly. "That's why I wanted to help, you know, with cleanin' the boots..."

Lieutenant Duffle looked serious. "Homemade fixes are no good at all, Tickle. It's only prayer and reading the Bible that properly prepare us to face the formidable enemies we might meet, and that teach us to behave in the right way to each other too. You can never clean your armour boots with anything less than the undiluted Water of Sound Doctrine."

Gamrie was silent at that. He was a young Christian and there was still a great deal for him to discover about Bible Truth; there was so much to study and understand to become a truly faithful Christian. Gamrie didn't yet know much about the Water of Sound Doctrine although he had certainly seen it. He pictured the deep, fathomless, fast-moving water that surrounded the city of Aletheia like a massive, flowing moat. It represented the whole truth of the Bible.

"If you can learn to properly prepare and wear your armour

of God for every day of your life as a Christian, you will make a great Rescuer," added Lieutenant Duffle.

Gamrie beamed. He immediately determined to do just that, but meanwhile something else had occurred to him. "Oh, sir… there's just one small thing, sir."

"Well?"

"You see, the Rescuer left so quickly, sir, well, you see, sir, I didn't get paid, sir!"

Recording the matter

Lieutenant Reuben Duffle was a methodical man. In the end, he walked all the way home with Gamrie and personally delivered him to his infuriated mother, *without* pay. The lieutenant gathered the distinct impression that this was not the first time, nor was it likely to be the last time, that young Tickle was in a scrape.

He returned to the Academy and ordered the washing of the sticky paving slabs that were the only remaining evidence of Gamrie Tickle's first proper enterprise in Aletheia.

Then he went to his office and wrote a note. Along with the date and the time, he penned the following words:

'Gamrie Tickle apprehended attempting to clean Trainee Dim View's boots on paving slabs at the front of the Academy. Forbidden further enterprise on Academy property. Returned to mother for action. Tickle expressed a keen interest in working

at the Academy. If interest continues, consider High School voluntary job.'

This was the first of many accounts placed in Gamrie Tickle's file.

THE BOOT CLEANER

Bible Verses

John 3:16:
'For God so loved the world that He gave His only begotten Son, that whoever believes in Him should not perish but have everlasting life.'

Ephesians 6:10-18:
'Finally, my brethren, be strong in the Lord and in the power of His might. Put on the whole armour of God, that you may be able to stand against the wiles of the devil. For we do not wrestle against flesh and blood, but against principalities, against powers, against the rulers of the darkness of this age, against spiritual hosts of wickedness in the heavenly places. Therefore take up the whole armour of God, that you may be able to withstand in the evil day, and having done all, to stand.

Stand therefore, having girded your waist with truth, having put on the breastplate of righteousness, and having shod your feet with the preparation of the gospel of peace; above all, taking the shield of faith with which you will be able to quench all the fiery darts of the wicked one. And take the helmet of salvation, and the sword of the Spirit, which is the word of God; praying always with all prayer and supplication in the Spirit...'

Bible Lesson: Be Prepared!

1. To become a Christian, a person must trust in the Lord Jesus to save them from the punishment they deserve for all the wrong things they have done. John 3:16 (above) is a verse which explains this.

2. Once you are a Christian you need to prepare, every day, to serve God. To be prepared as a Christian, you must put on the armour of God each day – by reading the Bible and praying to God for help and guidance. Each piece of armour represents something different. (You can read more about this in The Rescue of Timmy Trial, Aletheia Adventure Series Book 1).

3. As a Christian, you are individually responsible for preparing your 'armour' and putting it on every day. You can't rely on someone else to do this for you: you must personally learn to read the Bible and pray.

4. And remember – don't try and do things your own way (like Gamrie did with his DIY fixes!). Only the Bible, which is the Word of God, can truly prepare and guide and direct you. There is no other substitute.

2. UNDER THE STORM

The summer after Gamrie's experiment with boot-cleaning was a particularly hot one. Day after day the sun shone from a cloudless blue sky – until it was so hot that the farmers became anxious about their crops. The managers at the Academy of Soldiers-of-the-Cross were also concerned. They watched the machines in the fantastic Central Control Room of the Academy, wondering what was happening in the land of Err and why things were so worrying in Aletheia.

You see, if the people of Err were concocting a new way of attacking Aletheia, their wicked behaviour affected the things around them – trees and plants and food, creatures and machines, and most definitely the weather.

Having the right weather in Aletheia was very important for the crops to grow, and only food grown on the Pray-Always Farmlands was safe for the people of Aletheia to eat. That summer, the leaders of Aletheia began to wonder what the people of Err were doing that was affecting the crops of the Pray-Always Farmlands.

Now the best defence the people of Aletheia had was always prayer to God. Prayer power meant that they would be able to fend off trouble from the land of Err. But that summer people were growing weary under the wilting heat; they stopped praying as much. The dial on the big Prayer Power Monitor in the Control Room began to move rapidly from *Good*, downwards through *Sufficient*, yet farther downwards into *Adequate*, until it reached *Barely Adequate* before anyone knew what to do about it. Then people began to get sick too.

Have you ever heard people complain about the weather? It's too hot, or too cold, or too wet, or too dry…? The weather is this, and that, but whatever it tries to do, it's just not quite right. Complaining is not a particularly nice thing. Beware of moaning about anything too much: because, before you know where you are, prayer is down, and trouble is waiting to pounce on you! In Aletheia, a type of Moaning Mumps – which is a bit like the flu in our world – began to spread rapidly across the city with all the moaning and complaints. Even people who had never complained before were caught by it. Because if there is one thing that is *really contagious*, it's moaning!

What Gamrie did that summer

Gamrie was unaware of the concerns in Aletheia. He didn't complain at all. He amused himself outside all summer, impervious to the heat. Across the wide reaches of Aletheia, from one boundary to another, he roamed: chatting to the farmers busy in their fields; helping with one thing and another (until things went wrong and he was urged to go and help elsewhere); visiting the local shops, hotels, and anywhere else where there was unrestrained access; even visiting The Outskirts of Aletheia, interested in all the differences there, talking to whoever was about.

Now, I should explain that people who live on The Outskirts of Aletheia live away from the cross at the centre of Aletheia. They're Christians, but they often forget about the cross of the Lord Jesus and everything He did when He died to save us from our sins and bring us back to God. They forget how great God is and forget to be grateful and humble. They can become strict, or lazy, or fearful, or grumbling, or unkind, or doubting. They begin to make up their own rules for living; they begin to doubt the Bible; they no longer trust it to have the answers they need.

Gamrie was particularly intrigued with the people on The Outskirts who lived in Doubt Development. As you might have guessed, these people had their *doubts* about quite a few things. They weren't taken by surprise at the spread of Moaning Mumps that summer; they had always doubted that Aletheia was completely healthy and safe.

The odd thing about the people in Doubt Development was that, while they doubted bits about the Bible, they believed the most weird and wonderful alternatives. Gamrie found them fascinating because they invented such incredible things to dispel their doubts. They would try anything!

But more of this later in the story…

Aunt Tess

Tess Steady was pretty, young, and single. She was also Gamrie's aunt. She was not particularly like her lively, scatty, impulsive older sister Trixie (Gamrie's mother), but she did have a sense of humour, and she was very fond of her nephews and niece – Titus, Gamrie, and Tinkerbelle Tickle.

Tess had a small farm on the Pray-Always Farmlands. She had chickens, a few sheep, a couple of cows, an old donkey, a few cats, and two dogs. She grew potatoes and carrots and other vegetables, and had a wonderfully trim and tidy orchard containing a variety of fruit. There was a neat farmhouse, a barn, and a small pasture for the animals. It was very cosy and quaint – like something you might draw if you wanted to create a picture of the perfect little farm.

Next door to Tess lived Mr Thatch Straw. He had a much larger farm, and, whenever he could, he helped her out with the bigger tasks – such as harvesting potatoes and making hay, and anything else he could find to do. Tess was quite sure she could manage on her own, but Thatch liked an excuse to help her. Tess thought that he felt sorry for her, but actually he helped her because he liked her very much; in fact, he wanted to marry her. But Thatch was a shy man and he hadn't figured out how to tell her. Plenty of folk didn't think he ever would.

Things had gone on in this stable, but unsatisfactory, way for some time. But that summer something changed the quiet routine: Gamrie and his hazardous younger sister, Tinkerbelle, came to stay. This is how it came about.

Journey across Aletheia

A combination of unfortunate circumstances led to the particular adventure that Gamrie fell into that long, hot summer: The first was that Trixie Tickle, Gamrie's mother, fell ill with the Moaning Mumps. Teffle, Gamrie's father, was a quiet, sober-minded man who worked as a clerk in the serious, echoing corridors of the Judges' Academy. Gamrie's older brother, Titus, a sensible, studious boy, spent his summer studying and helping diligently around the house. But the thought of Gamrie, and his younger sister, Tinkerbelle, loose around the house while Trixie was so unwell, was far too much for the hardworking Teffle to contemplate. Gamrie was usually absent amusing himself around Aletheia, but Tinkerbelle – a flyaway, impulsive imp of a child who generally lived in a world of her own and could certainly cause as much chaos as Gamrie could – was everywhere and into everything at every moment of the day. So Gamrie and seven-year-old Tinkerbelle were dispatched to their Aunt Tess for the final two weeks of the holiday.

Gamrie went quite willingly. There was always something to see and do with Aunt Tess – the barn, the animals, the funny, quaint farmhouse with its unknown nooks and crannies, the hen coop, the orchard, the strawberry patch when the strawberries were ripe… possibilities were endless. Aunt Tess was fun too

– although she didn't stand much nonsense. She had a way, which no one else in his experience had, of anticipating his next move and putting a firm stop to any untoward adventures. But Gamrie was very fond of her.

Tinkerbelle – or Belle as she was known – went willingly wherever her brother Gamrie went. The two of them set off across the Pray-Always Farmlands to the small farm on the southern slopes of Aletheia. Belle skipped happily through the sunshine while her older, much bigger, brother carried the rucksack containing their belongings.

If Belle had one consistent feeling in her life, it was that she loved Gamrie. She laughed at his jokes, whether they were funny or not. She loved his stories. She admired his adventures. She admired *him*. She was always on his side in trouble. She would do anything he said.

For that reason, she didn't object when they went considerably out of their way on their journey to Aunt Tess. In fact, they walked west, not south at all, and took the very winding Unbelief Road that eventually led to the town of Doubt. They had been given money to get a gift for Aunt Tess on their way. "Buy her flowers," their sick mother suggested. "Something to make her feel nice. She so seldom has any time for such things. She's so busy, she must be so tired…"

Gamrie considered the matter seriously. He had no notion why flowers might make someone feel nice; he had a suspicion they wouldn't do *that* at all. He pondered silently on the matter for some time. "I don't see why," he said to Belle at last, "I don't see why we should *buy* her flowers when we can *pick* some on the way."

"Let's pick them!" agreed Belle eagerly.

Gamrie continued, "In fact, we could get something *much more* interesting for Aunt Tess."

"Much more interesting," echoed Belle.

Gamrie led the way and Belle followed. Belle would have followed him anywhere.

To Gamrie, the world around often appeared in shades of ambiguous grey: that is to say, when you said one thing to him, he would consider all possible alternative shades of meaning, apply his own interpretation, and quite often come up with something the opposite to what you intended. This is precisely what he did now.

On his extensive summer travels around Aletheia, he had heard that the Peddler on Unbelief Road would sell you cures and treatments for just about anything. In fact, he had met a man in Doubt Development who had bought a cure for stress and busyness. This man doubted what the Bible said about resting, and laying down burdens, and casting care on God; he didn't think that was the whole answer to the problem. So instead he bought some invigorating blue liquid and took a spoonful every night as instructed. And he was convinced it worked! He was less busy, less tired than before. He had found the cure! He didn't tell Gamrie the details. What actually happened was that the man slept an hour or two longer in the morning and didn't get as much done; the blue liquid was only a simple sleeping draught. Gamrie didn't ask any probing questions: he heard what he wanted, and he was impressed.

When they had walked the long, winding path of Unbelief Road for some time, at last they saw the bridge over the Water of Sound Doctrine that marked the boundary of Aletheia.

Gamrie hesitated.

All his life he had been taught the dangers of the land of Err, and as long as he could remember he had wanted to *just once* step outside the safety of Aletheia. On the other side of the bridge, easily within reach, a Peddler was standing behind a shabby table containing curious wares.

It was on the wrong side of the Water of Sound Doctrine.

Purchasing a gift

It didn't take long. Nothing drastic or untoward happened to Gamrie. Very quickly the purchase was made. Although the shining blue liquid was much more expensive than he had anticipated, Gamrie concluded that he hadn't especially needed the new schoolbook entitled 'Burden Bearing' that he had been instructed to read in the holidays. He didn't think 'burden bearing' was likely to get him any closer to being a Rescuer. The Peddler took all their money and, somewhat reluctantly, he took the 'Burden Bearing' book too.

Eventually, Gamrie and Belle were back on track and once more headed across the well-kept farmlands. Now they were heading south in the right direction. Behind them, glowering and menacing, a big storm filled the northern sky. Gamrie didn't worry much about that. In fact, he was occupied with something that was of much greater importance – the fact that he and his sister hadn't yet had lunch. Their money was gone; they were very hungry; Belle was beginning to tire.

Gamrie had some misgivings about being involved in a venture that included his little sister. He was fond of her, but was doubtful about the strict instructions he had received from his parents regarding his younger sibling and their good behaviour. What exactly did *looking after* her entail? He was often present when his parents tried to do precisely that and it was never, in his opinion, without a great deal of effort and grief. Now, with every step, she was asking how much farther they had to go.

"You've got to behave this time, Belle," he said gloomily, as he and his sister walked across the patchwork of Pray-Always Farmlands fields under the hot, glowering sun.

"Why?" asked Belle.

Gamrie considered. He wasn't actually sure why this time, in particular, their behaviour had been emphasised so much. He shrugged. "'Cos Mum's been ill, I guess that's why," he said. "And Aunt Tess is busy an' stuff on the farm. It's harvest. And 'cos I've got to look after you."

Belle said feelingly, "I wish you could always look after me!"

"I don't," said Gamrie bluntly.

"Why?"

"Wouldn't be much good at it," he replied with firm conviction.

"You would, you would, Gamrie…"

"Wouldn't do it," he said doggedly.

Belle sighed. "I would be good," she said coaxingly.

"No, you wouldn't," said Gamrie feelingly, remembering all the lectures his parents gave on the subject that seemed to have little effect.

Belle was silent for a spell.

Up ahead, their aunt's farmhouse was coming into view at last.

Suddenly Belle said, "You would miss me if I died, wouldn't you, Gamrie?"

Gamrie was thinking of lunch. He was wondering if his aunt had baked any of his favourite cookies. He was certain he could eat a whole batch…

"Died?" he echoed vaguely. "Of course you won't die!"

Gamrie was annoyed and hungry; Belle turned darkly mysterious. "You wait and see," she said. "Just you wait and see!"

A sudden fall

Tess Steady was usually up at the crack of dawn, and the morning of the expected arrival of her nephew and niece was no different. Summer was such a busy time, but she wouldn't have changed her work for any other job in the world. She headed out into the early morning sunshine to do her chores. It was another cloudless day, but on the horizon in the north a big storm was definitely brewing. It looked like a bad thunderstorm: dark and angry, black with streaks of threatening purple. Tess eyed it dubiously. There was still plenty of time to get the animals into the barn before the storm. The children could help too.

The cows stood patiently while they were milked. The sheep grazed peacefully. Trevor, the donkey, followed her around the field, wanting a nice scratch. If you looked south from Aletheia, it was like any other glorious summer morning; everything was sunshine and clear blue sky. If you looked north, the storm was already swallowing up the sky.

Thatch Straw's farm was also situated on the southern slopes of the Pray-Always Farmlands. He was up early working in his big hay field. He, too, had seen the storm. The dry, sweet-smelling hay he had cut must be gathered before the first rain fell. He already had the wagon well filled with the first load. He waved at Tess when he saw her. She blushed and waved back.

After lunch, the children still hadn't arrived, so Tess finished her afternoon chores and kept an eye on the now fast-approaching storm. She felt a little unwell. But she ignored the funny scratchy feeling in her throat and the faintness that was so unusual for her. She could *not* get ill! She could not succumb to the Moaning Mumps that had struck Aletheia. Not with all the potatoes to harvest, her small patch of grass to cut for hay, and the first of the apples ready to pick and store, to say nothing of the animals to tend, and her nephew and niece about to arrive. Perhaps the presence of Gamrie might, this time, prove a blessing. She could closely supervise him digging potatoes and turning the hay and doing the other heavy jobs. He was built a bit like an ox, and that, at least, had its advantages.

She brought the animals in early and made them comfortable in the barn. She brought the hens in too. Thatch was on his last load of hay. He waved at her again. She waved back. She hoped he might call later. Probably he would come and check up on her before the storm hit.

When the children at last arrived, she was high up a rickety old ladder collecting eggs from an errant hen who had escaped to the hay loft. She heard the gruff shout of Gamrie and the tinkling voice of Belle. Yip and Yap, her two collie dogs, were barking madly in the yard, no doubt capering around the children. She smiled.

"In here!" she called. "In the barn!" Her voice was croaky, her throat sore.

They quickly appeared in the doorway.

Gamrie said, "You sound funny." He immediately dumped the rucksack containing their belongings on the ground. He regarded his aunt with interest where she was, high up in the eaves of the barn.

"Can I come up there?" he asked.

"No, of course not! I'm just collecting eggs."

"I'd like to do that," said Belle, looking at the wonderfully tempting ladder.

"Tomorrow you can," said Aunt Tess, who pictured the safe nesting boxes in the ground level hen coop. She fleetingly wondered how much damage Belle could do there. Surely not much…

Tess put the eggs in the pockets of her work overalls and began to descend the old ladder. "Oh... oh dear..."

"What are you doin'?" asked Gamrie, watching as his aunt suddenly clutched the ladder with trembling fingers. The ladder shifted precariously. "You alright?" he added with unusual concern.

"I don't feel so well today..." Aunt Tess said faintly.

Gamrie suddenly understood precisely that.

"Is she going to fall?" Belle asked with detached interest, as Aunt Tess continued to clutch the feebly swaying ladder.

Gamrie made a swift decision. "I'll come and get you," he said.

"That's really not a good idea..." Aunt Tess spoke feebly, trying to clear the black shadows dancing in her eyes. Gradually everything was coming back into focus again. "Stay down. I'll be alright..."

But she was too late. The considerable bulk of Gamrie was already ascending the fragile ladder... and you can probably guess what happened next. From feeble swaying under the slight weight of Aunt Tess, the ladder suddenly gave up completely. It didn't like the weight of Gamrie at all! Down it came, *crashing* down, onto the barn floor. Gamrie tumbled in a heap and immediately sprang to his feet, dusting down his clothing and looking quite offended.

"It looked much stronger than that!" he said, eyeing the ladder indignantly.

Sprawled under the ladder lay the form of Aunt Tess. The

eggs were smashed under her. There was a cut on her head. She wasn't moving at all.

In awe, Gamrie approached the prone figure on the ground.

"Is she dead?" squeaked Belle. "Is she dead? Did you kill her, Gamrie?"

While his sister leapt around him, Gamrie knelt down by his aunt. He prodded her arm. "Um… Aunt Tess…? Aunt Tess…?"

There was no response.

Solemnly, he looked at his equally awestruck sister. "We've killed her," he said.

What happened to Aunt Tess?

Of course, the truth wasn't quite as dramatic as that or I would hardly dare tell you this tale. While the two collie dogs danced around, barking and perplexed, Gamrie managed to remove the ladder from his aunt. And then, to his unfathomable relief, Tess groaned.

"She's not dead! She's not dead! Belle, she's not dead!" he yelled to his sister.

Belle, who had gone to make a daisy chain wreath to mark her aunt's decease (obviously not comprehending how dreadful this event would have been had it been true), came running with daisies spilling from her dress.

"Of course I'm not dead!" said Aunt Tess, slowly sitting up. Fortunately she had landed on a deep, soft layer of straw. She was bruised, but that was all.

"Will you go to hospital?" asked Belle.

"And what will I do with you? Leave Trevor in charge?"

Knowing Trevor was the donkey, Belle giggled.

"Help me up, Gamrie…"

Gamrie grabbed her arm and once more Aunt Tess groaned. "I think I'm bruised," she said.

Between Gamrie's brute strength and Aunt Tess' determination she was soon on her feet – feeling oddly faint and wishing Gamrie wasn't quite as clumsy.

A loud rumble of thunder suddenly reverberated through the hot, still air.

"Quickly, to the house, children!"

They shut the barn up tight, then, propelled along by the strong, willing Gamrie, Tess made it to the house. They all entered the cosy kitchen.

Lightning split the sky. Another loud BANG of thunder shook the house.

"We made it just in time!" said Aunt Tess.

Aunt Tess was pretty cool. She ignored the gash on her head (actually, she didn't know it was there), and, to Gamrie's relief, she began to pull her cookie tin from the shelf and get glasses from the cupboard. She poured lovely, fresh lemonade for the children and made herself a strong cup of tea, hoping it would revive her.

Belle piped up, "We missed lunch."

"Missed lunch? Whatever were you doing?"

"We went the long way round to get here," remarked Gamrie.

"I'm sure you did," their aunt said knowingly.

She began to gather more food together. Gamrie watched her with fond gratitude. He really did like Aunt Tess! Then he remembered their gift. He rummaged in the rucksack, and then, into his aunt's dark tea, he liberally poured the blue liquid from the Peddler's bottle. This should cure everything. She actually *said* she didn't feel well. His mum said she was too busy and tired. The Peddler said this would fix all of that. He scrutinised the tea. You couldn't see anything had changed in the dark brew. What a lovely surprise for his aunt to be suddenly cured!

They ate their cookies and generous slices of homemade bread with thick lemon curd. Gamrie ate a lot very quickly, focussed intently and exclusively on food. When the last slice of bread was gone, and the last cookie eaten, he surveyed his aunt.

She had finished her tea.

At any moment the cure would work.

Something certainly seemed to be taking effect. There was a blue tinge around her mouth, which together with the gash on her head, made her look more like the victim of a nasty accident than the recipient of a miracle cure.

Then, without any warning, she slipped to the floor.

There was a thud.

Once more, she was still and lifeless.

Thatch Straw to the rescue

In the meantime, Thatch Straw, having made his own farm

secure, hurried across to Tess' house to see that everything was safe. Once more, lightning split the sky above Aletheia, and thunder crashed through the air. Dark, menacing clouds gathered and shifted uneasily in the sky above him. Any moment now, rain would start to fall.

To his surprise, a large, untidy boy met him at the door of Tess' neat farmhouse. Then he remembered: Tess' nephew and niece were coming to stay. The boy didn't seem particularly surprised to see the big farmer there, but he did look extremely relieved. Without preamble, he said, "You should come in. I think she's dead again!"

With a sudden shriek of fury, the storm broke on Aletheia. There were simply too many people suffering from Moaning Mumps to raise the prayer power to stop it. The wind came with the storm and bent the trees, beating them mercilessly as the rain began to lash the farmlands. Thatch, with thoughts only of his beloved Tess, horrified by what the boy had said, hurried into the kitchen... and there she was. Lying across the floor. White, still, unresponsive.

Thatch had doctored plenty of animals, and, while the boy explained about his aunt's fall from the ladder, he tried to see if there were any broken bones or other injuries besides the nasty gash on her head – but she seemed unhurt. Something was clearly amiss but her breathing was reassuringly deep and regular. Could it be a bad case of the Moaning Mumps? It hadn't quite reached the farmlands, and he didn't think that Tess, who never complained, was likely to catch it anyway.

Besides, he had never heard of anyone collapsing with the Moaning Mumps. They had all been warned of the symptoms – and he was quite sure this wasn't one of them. What *was* that blue tinge on her lips? That surely wasn't a good sign! Either way, it was beyond him. She needed urgent medical treatment.

The storm raged, growing moment by moment like a wild animal. Thatch had never seen anything like it before. But even the damage the storm might cause to his beloved farmlands was nothing to his concern for Tess. He knew he could not get her safely through the storm to the Academy of Soldiers-of-the-Cross for the treatment she needed. There was only one way to reach help.

He turned abruptly to the watching boy. "We need to go underground," he said. "You'll have to come too."

If he expected any objection, he was happily mistaken. Gamrie's eyes lit up. "I've always wanted to go into underground Aletheia!" he said.

About underground Aletheia

If you've read *The Defenders of Aletheia* you will already know about underground Aletheia. Although it's beneath the ground, and in places it's dark and mysterious, it's actually a rather interesting, even welcoming, place.

You see, the whole of Aletheia – all the important buildings in the centre of the city, and all the farms across the Pray-Always Farmlands, have access to the foundations underneath Aletheia. The massive stone walls of city buildings reach far,

far under the surface to form safe, secure shelters. All the city centre streets are duplicated below the aboveground streets.

The farms are a little less accessible because they're farther away. But Mr Straw knew his best hope of finding help for Tess lay in taking her through the streets under the ground, to doctors at the Academy of Soldiers-of-the-Cross.

Journey underground

Thatch Straw knew exactly where Tess' underground entry hatch was. He removed his Bible from the pouch at his side, and fitted it to the book-shaped indentation on the hatch. There was a soft, reassuring *click*. Thatch opened the hatch. Then he fetched a warm throw from the living room sofa, wrapped the unresponsive Tess up securely, and returned to the hatch with her. He noticed the boy clutching a piece of paper, which he quickly stuck in his pocket. Thatch didn't ask any questions; Tess was the main concern. And he was grateful for the willing cooperation of the strong lad when he carried Tess and her blanket down the steep ladder underground.

Once the ladder ended, they were in a long, earth-walled passageway. There were no street lamps here, but Thatch opened his Bible and balanced it in one hand as he held Tess in his arms. It shone brightly through the passageway, lighting the way they had to go.

Gamrie exclaimed, "I never saw the Bible shine so brightly before!"

"The Bible is always a light to those who believe," said Thatch. He moved his Bible and Tess shifted and sighed in his arms. Then she settled back into her deep, impenetrable, unconscious slumber.

Gamrie knew the Bible shone as a light. In Aletheia, they were taught that from their earliest years. *'Your word is a lamp to my feet and a light to my path'* was a Bible verse he had learned at school, and in Aletheia this verse was literally true. The Bible showed real, physical light for people who believed in it.

Thatch explained, "The Bible will give as much light as we allow it to give through our belief, our faith in it. The more you believe and are trusting in it, the more light you're shown."

Gamrie was now thinking of another matter. Suddenly he said, "You really like her, don't you?" He watched the big farmer taking such good care of his aunt. There was something very particular about it. Had he been especially observant (and he was *not*), he would have noticed the reddening of Thatch's cheeks.

Thatch didn't reply. He walked on, lengthening his stride.

Gamrie wasn't one to take obvious hints, let alone subtle ones. He jogged to keep up and prompted, "Don't you like her? I thought most people liked her, you see…"

Thatch said sternly, "That's private," in a most discouraging tone.

"*Private*?" Gamrie was amazed. "Why? She's alright for an aunt," he continued, without waiting for an answer. "She's fun and stuff, but quite strict too. If you married her, you could have two farms," he added reflectively.

Thatch muttered, "That would *not* be a good enough reason to marry."

Gamrie shrugged. "Wouldn't it?" It wasn't something he had considered. "She needs someone to take care of her too," he suggested. "Like now. She was nearly dead, wasn't she? But you rescued her!"

Thatch had nothing to say about that either.

"Belle wants her to be married so she can…" Gamrie trailed off. He looked sideways at the tough, capable farmer. His bright blue eyes were suddenly enlightened. "I think I know what it means now!" he said suddenly.

Not much of Gamrie's conversation made sense. Thatch wasn't inclined to question him about whatever urgent matter he was now contemplating.

Gamrie lapsed into thoughtful silence. He was in awe of underground Aletheia and there was plenty to distract him. For a while he scanned his surroundings eagerly. He regretted their haste. It gave him no opportunity to explore the intriguing nooks and crannies, and twist and turns, and passageways snaking this way and that, and sign posts pointing and naming interesting places. Tree roots entwined through the roof and walls of the passages. Thatch moved unerringly through the labyrinth of tunnels, neither hesitating or slowing.

"Oh, Mr Straw, sir…" Slightly desperately, Gamrie caught up with the hurrying figure. "I think I know what it means now! I think I know where she's gone, you see?"

Thatch didn't see at all. He shifted Tess in his arms and moved the light of the Bible. As he did so, a few of those brilliant rays fell across her and once more she seemed wakeful. But then she sank back into deep sleep again.

As they moved on, the passageway went uphill and the earth walls gradually gave way to rock, and then to proper carved stone walls. The darkness ceased and friendly streetlamps lined the way. These weren't exactly like the streetlamps you might see where you live – because in each of these lamps there was a Bible, brightly shining to show people the way. There were doors and windows, and the thick walls of deep, secure foundations. It was quiet here. There were no people about. You see, Aletheians weren't intended to live out of sight in the shadows. The foundations of the city were kept firm and secure, but only in a real emergency did people retreat underground.

Gamrie once more hurried to keep pace with Thatch's long stride. "About my sister, sir…"

Thatch didn't break stride. "Your sister?"

"It's just that… it's just that I think… I think she's lost… lost down here, you see, sir?" The last bit all came out in a hurry – as if he was spilling a desperate secret that was suddenly too much to bear.

Thatch stopped abruptly in horrified astonishment. Suddenly it struck him that Tess had said something about her nephew *and niece* coming to stay. A small child, a rascal, Tess had said affectionately…

Thatch asked, "Your sister went through the underground entry before us?"

"I think so, sir…"

"She managed to open the underground entry with her Bible?"

Gamrie had absolutely no idea about this. "I think she must have, sir." He screwed up his face in concentration. "She left a note you see, sir…"

"A note!" Thatch had a fleeting recollection of this boy sticking a piece of paper in his pocket. "And you only think to tell me now?! What does the note say?"

Since Belle was only seven, the note didn't make a great deal of sense. The words 'hide', 'me', and 'find' were clear enough; Gamrie filled in the gaps with his own interpretation of events.

"I think it's 'cos she wanted me to find her," said Gamrie. "She said somethin' about missing her if she died…"

"If she *died*?" echoed Thatch, utterly bewildered.

"Earlier when we were walkin'… '*wait and see*', she said… '*wait and see*'… I 'spect she's played a trick on us!"

Thatch had no idea when he had become part of the '*us*' the child had played a trick on. What he *did* know was that now he had a missing child and an unconscious woman to deal with. Besides one very frustrating boy!

Once more, Tess stirred.

Thatch suddenly realised what was affecting her deep, unconscious state: it was the light of the Bible. Its beams moved with the movement of his hand. Any stray ray seemed on the point of waking her. He lifted the light of the Bible and shone its bright, radiant, healing beams across her face. After a moment her eyes blinked open. She stared at him in bewilderment.

"Thatch?" she faltered. "I had such a strange dream…!"

Solving the puzzle

Quickly, Tess fully revived. Gamrie noticed some strange, secret, happy whispered exchanges between the farmer and his aunt. They seemed to have an awful lot to say to each other. Thatch put her down, but he still had his arm about her. They were acting as if they *really loved* each other now!

He muttered to himself, "I *knew* he liked her! It's not *private* after all!" Adults were so weird and silly sometimes.

After a short discussion, in which Gamrie was not asked for his opinion, it was decided they would continue to the Academy of Soldiers-of-the-Cross, which was a short distance ahead. They needed to fetch help. Even if Tess no longer required medical attention – she insisted she was fine – there was now a missing child to find. By now, Belle might be anywhere.

They reached the Academy without further delay. Rescuers were dispatched to start searching the underground of Aletheia for Belle. Thatch insisted that a doctor examine Tess. Gamrie wished he could explore his surroundings. At last he had gained admittance to the Academy of Soldiers-of-the-Cross! But Aunt Tess seemed to anticipate his desire to wander.

"You stay with us, Gamrie!" she said firmly.

Mr Straw seconded this with a stern frown.

Gamrie sighed and followed.

"I don't know what came over me," Tess said to the doctor. "I felt a bit unwell earlier, and I had the fall... I thought it might be the Moaning Mumps. But suddenly everything went black. It was as if I was sleeping, but then I heard voices..."

A nurse cleaned the gash on Aunt Tess' head. The doctor examined her throat; took her temperature; listened to her heartbeat. Thatch held her hand.

At last the doctor said, "It's definitely not the Moaning Mumps. What you describe, and the reaction to the light of the Bible, leads me to think you absorbed some foreign substance from the land of Err."

Tess was puzzled. "I don't see how..."

"Have there been any strangers about? Any at all? Any changes in your diet or your routine...?"

Tess' still-tired mind suddenly cleared.

"There is one change in my routine today," she said slowly. She turned to her nephew. "Gamrie, did you put something, anything, on my cookie, or on the bread, or..."

"No," said Gamrie promptly. "'Course not! I wouldn't do that. But there *was* the gift we brought you."

"Gift...?"

"For you workin' so hard and being tired and stuff..."

Thatch asked sharply, "What gift?"

Gamrie huffed another sigh. Mr Straw seemed unreasonably

suspicious that it was all his fault! It wasn't as if he had done anything wrong. All he had tried to do was help his aunt get better. And he didn't think Mr Straw should act as if he *owned* Aunt Tess.

Aunt Tess prompted, "What gift, Gamrie?" in her no-nonsense voice.

Gamrie thought of the wonderful blue bottle for which he had paid such a high price. "The man called it Restorative Re-Repose."

Following his revelation, the suspicion he had excited exploded into full-blown blame and Gamrie had reason to be grateful for his aunt and Mr Straw's distraction with each other. They soon forgot about him…

What about Belle?

The discovery of Belle turned out to be quite a simple matter. The troops of Rescuers, who systematically searched the underground through the ferocious storm, found nothing at all. Later that evening, when the storm had ended, when Thatch had escorted Tess and Gamrie back to the farmhouse and then left for his own home, Belle crept through to the kitchen from a long snooze in her aunt's bed. She had forgotten she had been hiding from Gamrie. She was rested and refreshed from her exhausting walk across Aletheia. All she really wanted to know was, "Is it time for tea yet?"

A happy ending

Before we leave Thatch Straw and Tess Steady, I'll briefly explain what happened next. They were married later that year. People afterwards joked that it took something as devastating as the unpredictable presence of Gamrie Tickle to bring them together at last. But perhaps it would have happened anyway.

Gamrie was not aware of his unintentional part in uniting the happy couple. At this stage in his life, serious romance passed him by as an inevitable inconvenience and embarrassment for adults. It was not, yet, part of his pathway.

One more thing: you might be interested to know Thatch and Tess Straw had a son called Croft Straw. If you've read *The Mustardseeds* you'll know exactly who I mean!

UNDER THE STORM

Bible Verse

Psalm 119:105:
'Your word is a lamp to my feet
And a light to my path.'

[This doesn't mean that the Bible is a literal light; this verse is saying that the Word of God will be our guide through life if we believe what the Bible says.]

Bible Lesson – Follow Light!

1. In order to go in the right direction, we must follow the light. As Christians, this means using the teaching of the Word of God, the Bible, as our guide. The more we place our confidence and trust in it, the more it will reveal to us about the will of God and what we should do.

2. There are plenty of people offering advice about life and how we should live – such as the Peddler selling his wares! But beware of any solutions to problems in life that aren't in keeping with the teaching of the whole Bible.

3. Like the Moaning Mumps, complaining about things is very contagious! Remember how dangerous it is to have a moaning attitude – including moaning about things in Christian and church life. Prayer and thanksgiving can help us stop moaning.

4. Living on The Outskirts – away from the cross of the Lord Jesus – always puts a Christian at risk of not appreciating the whole Truth of the Word of God. Remember the sacrifice of the Lord Jesus and what He did to save us from our sins; focussing on His sacrifice will help to keep us right.

3. IT COULD HAPPEN TO ANYONE

Lieutenant Reuben Duffle was quickly promoted through the ranks of Rescuers. One day he would be Chief of Aletheia, but when Gamrie Tickle was at High School Lieutenant Duffle was appointed to the rank of First Lieutenant, responsible to the Captain of the Rescuers, Ritchie Steadfast. Lieutenant Duffle had certainly not forgotten the occasion when a young boy used treacle to clean a Trainee Rescuer's boots. Nor had he forgotten an incident the previous summer that led to a considerable number of Rescuers scouring underground Aletheia for a missing child.

However, because he was a very busy man, he was not aware that the boy involved on both of these occasions was now a High School student, as keen as ever on becoming a Rescuer, and just now starting voluntary work at the Academy.

Queenie Staple

Officer Queenie Staple was in charge of High School students and other volunteers who were keen to help around the gigantic fortress that was the Academy of Soldiers-of-the-Cross. She was also responsible for the General Supplies Department. Often, the students in her charge helped order, count, carry, deliver, unload, and organise all the miscellaneous supplies that were needed in the vast Academy.

Queenie Staple was a capable, no-nonsense woman who had a great memory for detail. If there were, at the last count, 296 paperclips in the cupboard on the fourth floor, she would wonder why you wrote 292 in your report, and where, in the massive castle, the missing four were. She wasn't mean – she simply wanted to account for every last detail. Her personal motto was: *'Nothing is too unimportant to be overlooked in the defence of Aletheia; not even a paperclip.'*

Queenie didn't forget people either. She had gone to school with Trixie Steady – now Trixie Tickle, after her marriage – and had no trouble remembering the tricks and mischief Trixie got up to. Trixie was always cheerful, always laughing, always walking right into trouble. So when she spotted the name 'Gamrie Tiberius Tickle' on her list of new volunteers, she had no problem making the connection. "Trixie's son," she thought. "I wonder if he takes after his mother…"

The Vomitorium

Among the many and varied nooks and crannies and places in the vast Academy was the Vomitorium. I don't imagine you have a Vomitorium in your house, and it doesn't *sound* pleasant, does it? But it really wasn't as dreadful as it sounds. In actual fact, it was the most incredible recycling system you could imagine: certainly much more advanced than anything you have where you live today, no matter how many coloured bins and containers you use!

The thick, rich, earthy-smelling sludge in the Vomitorium all came from safe, wholesome sources on the Pray-Always Farmlands – such as grass cuttings, and vegetable and fruit peelings. It was very important that nothing entered the cauldrons and giant mixing bowls but Pray-Always substance. You see, what was put *in*, determined what came *out*.

Everything was collected, and mixed, and scrutinised by a team of serious-minded scientists. Around and about the walls of the vast space were charts, gleaming test tubes, and glass-encased dials with large, complicated faces. These recorded the amounts of protein, fat, vitamins, minerals, fibre and so on that were contained in the massive cauldron. They analysed other things too – things that we can't discover so easily in our world – such as kindness, goodness, faithfulness, and peace that had gone into the produce.

The contents of the Vomitorium were used to fertilise the farmlands of Aletheia – a bit like garden compost. It was also used to provide additional nutrition for the animals of Aletheia. Everything was gathered, and then sorted. First, it was all collected in the big, central cauldron. Next, it was examined and treated. Lastly, it was distributed. Some went skimming down the funnel to the farmlands' fertiliser container. Some went flying down the chute for high-protein cows' feed. Some went down a tube for pigs. Other bits were for sheep and goats and so on. And so, the whole of the Vomitorium worked to provide goodness for the lands and animals of Aletheia.

Gamrie and Dismay

Gamrie was delighted when he was dispatched to take fresh supplies to the Vomitorium. He had no idea what the Vomitorium entailed, but it sounded intriguing, and a trip through the corridors of the Academy was definitely more exciting than counting pencils in the stationery cupboard on the ground floor. The trouble with counting pencils was that every time he counted, he reached a different answer.

"Stop putting them back in the box we're counting from!" snapped Dismay Defeatia, his fellow-student and colleague.

Gamrie wasn't put up or down by his companion. Everyone in school knew Dismay always saw the worst in everything. He wasn't sure why she was volunteering at the Academy. All she would say was that she wanted to "see behind the scenes."

"I keep forgetting which box is which," he said cheerfully. "How many pencils did you make it that time?"

"How can I make it *anything at all* when you keep counting from the pile that's already been counted, and putting them into the box we're counting from?" cried the exasperated Dismay.

"Well then, what number did you reach that time?"

"What difference does that make? How can I…?"

"I got to twenty-nine that time and…"

Dismay glared at him. "I only got to nineteen, and then you started to put them…!"

"Well, if we split it between twenty-nine and nineteen, we could put, let's see... about twenty-four? Shall we put twenty-four on the form?"

"How can you do *that*? You should let me be in charge and do it my way, and then..."

At this juncture a cool, calm voice interrupted. "I think, perhaps, the form should remain blank until the pencils have been accurately counted," said Queenie Staple. "You can return to this tomorrow, and I *will be* checking your results personally. We *do not* allow mere guess work in the important work of the Academy."

Dismay muttered darkly, "I knew that!"

Gamrie was astonished. Never in his wildest dreams did he imagine pencils were important. Then another thought occurred to him. "But, if you're counting them anyway, perhaps we don't need to..." he began, anxious to escape the pencils and his grim-faced companion.

"You will return and do this properly," repeated Queenie firmly. "But, for now, I have another task for you."

At that moment, Gamrie would have been happy with any alternative whatsoever. So, when Officer Staple asked them to go to the Vomitorium with additional supplies that were urgently required, he could have jumped for joy.

On the way to the Vomitorium

"I don't see why I should carry *all* the clean coats," grumbled

Dismay, as they clattered down the corridor.

Gamrie said matter-of-factly, "I would get 'em dirty before we got there. *She* said so." He gestured vaguely to the now empty passageway behind them – in the direction Officer Staple had taken.

Gamrie swung the mop and empty bucket wildly up and down, almost catching Dismay.

"Would you *stop*...!"

"Sorry," he said immediately. He examined the sealed plastic container of bright red liquid he held in his other hand. "I s'ppose it's cleaning stuff," he said. "What with all the sick an' stuff there must be down there..."

"Sick...!"

"The *Vomit*orium," he said with a grin. "Stacks and stacks of *sick*!"

"That's disgusting!"

Gamrie shrugged. He didn't mind if there was lots of vomit.

"Why are they green anyway?" Dismay poked at the neatly folded garments she clutched.

"It's 'cos of the sick, of course," he said gleefully. "I've got a good joke I made up about..."

Dismay was adamant. "I don't want to know! I'm sick to death of your jokes...!"

But her rebuke was cut short by his peals of laughter. "*Sick* to death! *Sick* to death! Get it? You do get it, don't you? You've just made a joke about *sick*...!"

"You're not even a tiny bit, *not one tiny bit* funny!" she said.

But he laughed on.

When they came to the massive spiral staircase at the heart of the Academy, Gamrie looked longingly at the gleaming Stair-Gobbler capsule that was at their level.

"What I wouldn't give to ride in *that*," he said wistfully. "Wouldn't you like to...?"

"No, I wouldn't," snapped Dismay. "And you know perfectly well that we're not allowed on the Stair-Gobbler unless we're with a trained Rescuer..." Dismay repeated the rules they had learned; she liked rules.

Gamrie dreamed of the day he could ride the Stair-Gobbler all by himself.

At the Vomitorium

Because they had to go the long way around, and not by way of the speedy Stair-Gobbler, there were plenty of opportunities to get delayed. They stopped frequently so that Gamrie could look at things, and got lost twice because they disagreed about directions. They arrived at the Vomitorium about twenty minutes after their expected time.

"Who are you?" asked a small, bespectacled man, startled to suddenly notice two young people on the viewing platform of the Vomitorium. Hands on hips, the man looked up at them.

"We're here with the supplies," said Dismay. She was wrinkling her nose at the pungent aroma all around them.

"Supplies... Oh, the urgent supplies we sent for! But that

was surely a good half hour ago. We managed without, we thought we were forgotten, but, well, let's have them then." He waved a hand as if he expected them to fall from the viewing platform at his feet, but instead, to their surprise, the platform began to descend.

In a short space of time, they were level with the man. They stepped from the platform onto the actual floor of the gigantic Vomitorium itself. The label on the man's immaculate green coat read, 'Spark Bunsen, Vomitorium Heating Engineer'.

"Well," said Mr Bunsen, "what do you have for us?"

"We have…" Dismay began to hastily explain. She wanted to complete their mission and return to the large, fresh-smelling places of the Academy as soon as possible.

But Gamrie wasn't remotely interested in their simple errand of delivering supplies. He was staring around the vast Vomitorium as he had been ever since they first arrived: at the massive central cauldron, at the chutes, and funnels, and tubes snaking in and out of the largest cauldron to other huge circular containers. Each one was a slightly different hue: rich dark earth, chocolate brown, the green-brown of early autumn, the red-brown of fallen leaves, the caramel-brown of melted toffee. What it would be like to work here! Gamrie instantly decided it was his dream job. In awe, he asked,

"Do you set all the temperatures and stuff?"

"That's me in a nutshell," said the man happily. He scanned his surroundings lovingly, content with the steady bubbling, the steam snaking slowly from one pot and more quickly from another. "You see the controls?" He pointed to a vast panel behind a glass-encased corridor that protected the instruments all around the sides of the room. "I set the temperatures, and monitor, and check, and re-check, and adjust them... me and Flame and Lava. Look, I'll show you..." He led the way to the panels, beginning an impromptu tour of the Vomitorium as if it were the finest palace in the world. "I'm on duty today, of course, and we had a slight spill. Soilia and Compostér got covered in the raw potato peelings that were going through the first processer. I suppose it could have been worse, we were due a load of chicken manure this afternoon... but we're fresh out of clean coats. That's why..."

Dismay hastily stepped forward and deposited the clean coats into the arms of Spark Bunsen. "Here are the coats. We should go now!"

He bundled them up and stuck them under his arm. "Well, thank you, young lady. We'll make use of these sooner or later, you can be sure. Always an accident waiting to happen around here..."

Dismay hissed, "Gamrie! Let's go!"

"Now, here we have..." Mr Bunsen turned to explain the complicated instrument panel before which he had stopped. But he looked around to discover that the boy who had been there one minute was most definitely gone the next. "Where is he?" he asked. "Where is your companion?"

"GAMRIE!" shouted Dismay, startling Mr Bunsen considerably with the volume she achieved. "GAMRIE, get here AT ONCE!"

A head poked up, barely visible above the height of the central cauldron. A distant voice said, "I *am* here!"

Mr Bunsen wiped his brow. "You mustn't wander off, boy," he said. It was all very well having an appreciative audience to whom he could explain the wonders of his beloved Vomitorium, but there were strict rules governing visitors, and the rules definitely *didn't* allow for school students to wander at will around the finely tuned cauldrons. Any slight variation in temperature or in a multitude of other variables, and all sorts of chaos could ensue! Why, one year... but that didn't bear thinking about.

Mr Bunsen's mild manner mustered authority. "Come back here, young man! You *must* stay by me and don't touch *anything...*"

Gamrie began to thread his way back around the central cauldron, looking longingly at the contents as he passed. Indignantly he explained, "Of course I wouldn't touch anything. I wouldn't do that! I would *like* to touch it, but..."

"Well, *you* would like to do that, wouldn't you!" muttered Dismay crossly. "That would be just like *you*! Now, *let's go...*"

"Watch OUT!" cried Mr Bunsen.

Gamrie was watching the contents of the dark, mesmerising cauldron. He clutched the mop and bucket... and managed, quite easily as it happened, to entangle his feet and legs in them... and went sprawling full length on the ground! The bucket shot from him and skidded across the floor, coming to rest against the side of the protective glass screen. The mop flipped up into the air, turning over and over like a well-practised acrobat. Down, down it came towards the cauldron. It hit the edge with a sharp *CLANG!*...

...and landed safely on the floor.

Through the background murmur of quiet bubbling, the loud clatter of the mop and bucket echoed around. Dismay smothered a giggle of enjoyment as Gamrie fell. Then out rushed Mr Bunsen from behind the glass partition.

"Get up, boy!" he cried. "Get up at once!" He was wild with concern at the very near miss this clumsy boy had precipitated. If even *one* foreign object entered a cauldron it could change the entire behaviour of the liquid. It could cause...

"I'm alright! I'm alright!" Gamrie got to his feet and dusted himself down. "No need to panic! I'm fine, everything is fine..." With his usual cheerful optimism he surveyed the scene: the mysterious cauldrons that he would so like to even *touch*; the smirking Dismay; the poor, panicked Mr Bunsen who was gesturing wildly at everything around.

"It's not *you* I'm worried about!" Mr Bunsen hardly spared him a glance as he rushed past him to the central, most important cauldron. He ascended the metal steps to the small viewing platform that was directly above the cauldron itself. Gamrie wished he had noticed that elevated position earlier. He would love to stand there, looking down into the heart of the mass of oozing stuff. Why, Mr Bunsen could even reach down with that ladle-like rod and gather a sample...

Through the quiet of the gigantic room, there came a horrified, anguished cry from Spark Bunsen. The first syllables were unintelligible. But they quickly became discernible. "What... in? What did... in? BOY! What did you put in?!"

"Put in?" asked Gamrie, interested but astonished. "Put in *there*?" He had retraced his steps to the central cauldron, glad to have any excuse to return to it. "I wouldn't put anything in *there*!" he added. "I only went to *look*! Not to put anything..." He trailed off into silence. A great change was occurring in the calm, thick, black liquid. Smaller, and then bigger, bubbles of alarming red began to disturb the dark surface.

Pop!

There! A small bubble, quickly vanishing away.

POP!

"A big 'un!" cried Gamrie, quite excited by the unexpected development. "There! Over there! Did you see it?"

A groan from poor Spark Bunsen was the only response. Then, fiercely, "What Did You Put In It, Boy? Tell... Me... QUICKLY!"

"But I really didn't, sir! I didn't..."

"Oh yes, you did!" Unnoticed, Dismay arrived on the scene. "That bright red cleaning liquid! It flew into the cauldron when you fell over!" There was something a bit nasty about the way Dismay said it; as if she was glad Gamrie had been so clumsy.

"Cl-cleaning l-l-liquid...?" stammered Mr Bunsen, the colour draining from his face. "A ch-chemical compound, now in the mixing cauldron...?"

Gamrie's face cleared. "I completely forgot! Of course! The

cleaning liquid! At least that's what we thought it was. We were bringing it to you as you asked for it, and it must have, well, come out of my hand when I fell over, and…"

But Mr Bunsen was no longer listening. Even Dismay had suddenly lost the momentary triumph of Gamrie's disaster. The black mass was turning increasingly to angry red, moving with barely concealed annoyance, as if it was about to…

"Back to the safety glass! RUN! QUICKLY! N-OO-WWW!!" yelled Mr Bunsen.

Run they did. Dismay with unthinking panic; Mr Bunsen with knowing terror; Gamrie with reluctance and one last, admiring, lingering glance.

His hesitation meant that Gamrie was the last to reach the shelter of the protective, reinforced glass. The mass of thick, oozing red liquid erupted just before he took cover. It was on Gamrie that the first drop fell: a splatter of thick, dark red landed on his shoulder. It slid down his arm, marking his sleeve like a jagged, ugly wound.

But far worse was to follow…

What followed…

It was like taking the lid off a very angry volcano. The explosion shook the thick walls of the Vomitorium: it smashed glass casings, splintered tubes, shattered cogs, destroyed needles and dials and sent them spinning in every direction. It split a couple of large pipes – which happily joined the chaos, squirting their contents into neighbouring cauldrons where they didn't belong. In every direction, on every conceivable thing, the crimson liquid rained. Saturated valuable instruments. Polluted every cauldron. Simply covered *everything*.

The protective glass screen, behind which Mr Bunsen, Dismay, and Gamrie crouched, did not break entirely apart. Wide cracks appeared, but the three of them were largely protected from the spewing mass of stodgy red.

It was an event that would not soon be forgotten in the history of the Academy. Lieutenant Reuben Duffle received an urgent summons to manage the emergency situation. When he and several senior managers at last surveyed the dripping, oozing liquid red that lined the entire Vomitorium, he quickly spotted an untidy, bulky boy standing with a sullen-looking girl. The boy had grown considerably, but there was no mistaking the boot-cleaner of a few years ago.

Gamrie Tickle was once more the centre of attention.

Could it happen to anyone?

Gamrie Tickle and the girl were standing by Mr Spark Bunsen. Mr Bunsen was answering questions and wringing his hands in anguish; the poor man was distraught. As for Gamrie, he appeared subdued but interested in the incredible destruction by which he was surrounded.

Lieutenant Duffle approached as the boy, too, was questioned.

"Just an accident," said Gamrie. "I'm very sorry, sir, but I simply tripped. Honestly, it could happen to anyone!"

No more pencils

It didn't come as a surprise to anyone apart from Gamrie himself that he was no longer allowed to go anywhere near the Vomitorium. Gamrie didn't understand their reasoning: after all, an accident could surely happen to anyone. Officer Queenie Staple also requested that he should be immediately removed from her jurisdiction and from anything to do with the General Supplies Department. She would not risk another incident upsetting her careful arrangements. With no regret, Dismay Defeatia watched him go. They would never be friends. As for Gamrie, he wasn't at all concerned that he was leaving the General Supplies Department. He sincerely hoped he would never count pencils again.

IT COULD HAPPEN TO ANYONE
Bible Verses
Ephesians 6:6-8: 'As bondservants of Christ, doing the will of God from the heart, with good will doing service, as to the Lord... knowing that whatever good anyone does, he will receive the same from the Lord...' **Deuteronomy 6:17**: 'You shall diligently keep the commandments of the Lord your God, His testimonies, and His statutes which He has commanded you.'

Bible Lesson – Be Careful!

1. Remember Gamrie's carelessness with the cleaning fluid in the Vomitorium? It was such a small thing, but there were drastic consequences! The Bible teaches us to be careful and diligent in God's service. This applies in every aspect of our daily lives. How careful and diligent we are in small, everyday matters will have an impact on far bigger things. For example, being diligent in reading our Bibles and praying every day will form a habit which will gradually have a good effect on the whole of our lives.

2. Gamrie wasn't really interested in the importance of the Vomitorium and what it did for Aletheia – he only wanted to please himself. Whatever we do in God's service should be done from the heart – in other words, we should always want to do it to please God. We shouldn't be doing things to please ourselves or impress others, but because we know that what we're doing is right before God and will please Him.

3. Carelessness can lead to contamination – if we're not careful about keeping ourselves right daily in Christian life, we can allow other things into our lives that ought not to be there. We can easily be contaminated if we feed on anything that is not based firmly on the teaching of the Bible.

4. And remember, as the explosion in the Vomitorium was caused by carelessness and affected the entire Academy, so our own careless conduct can have an effect on other people – not just on ourselves.

4. THE GRUMBLE-FLIES

Following discussion among various senior managers, it was decreed that Gamrie should stay away from volunteering at the Academy of Soldiers-of-the-Cross and concentrate on his school work and studies. They hoped that if, or when, he returned he would be more steady and reliable.

In actual fact, Gamrie did little study: as little as he possibly could. But a year after the incident at the Vomitorium, he discovered a project that interested him very much indeed.

Little did the students and schoolchildren of Aletheia, least of all Gamrie, know how tricky that summer was for the great city of Bible Truth. In contrast to the hot summer that brought on the Moaning Mumps, this one was wet and cold. Harvest was late and farmers feared it would be poor; people complained.

As you know, how people act in Aletheia and the land of Err has a dramatic effect on the weather and on all sorts of other things. That summer, because people were grumbling, there was a slow, steady, infiltration of pesky Grumble-Flies into the city. These are very small, excessively annoying insects – like the midges that are found in the Highlands of Scotland.

You can probably guess why the Grumble-Flies came and

how they thrived: they congregated and multiplied where people grumbled, feeding on complaints as if they were their favourite treats! They came in dark, shifting clouds. Hovering and buzzing. Biting and stinging and tormenting. They made nests in shrubs and bushes and trees in people's gardens. They even had colonies underground. When all the best spots were taken outside and underground, they began to move into the walls and roofs of buildings. The more people grumbled about them and their dreadful buzzing and biting, the more the Grumble-Flies multiplied. It was as if they had asked all their friends and relatives from the entire land of Err to come and have a holiday in damp, despairing Aletheia!

I'm sure you can imagine how the people of Aletheia felt: they were *extremely* fed up. Almost before the leaders of Aletheia were aware that the Grumble-Flies had started to arrive, there was already a large-scale invasion. The flies were simply everywhere.

Have you ever tried to be thankful for something when you're grumbling? It's pretty hard to do. Quite often something like grumbling starts small. It doesn't seem much at all... until it's too late to stop it and it's driven all the thankfulness from you; then you don't feel grateful for anything at all. The last thing you want to do is pray. The grumbling people of Aletheia didn't pray as much. They no longer felt thankful to God for all the wonderful things they had received. Instead all they could think about was the dreadful weather and the terrible Grumble-Flies.

You'll know by now that Christians *not praying* is a very serious situation. The power of the city of Aletheia – the people they could rescue, the food they needed from the Pray-Always Farmlands, even their protection as a city – relied on people praying. That summer the situation became serious, and Chief Wiseman and the leaders and managers of Aletheia knew that something must be done. They searched the Bible, and searched the history and information books in the Judges' Academy. There was no record of such a large-scale invasion of Grumble-Flies. Some of the leaders were tempted to grumble about *that*: but that would only make the matter worse! So they prayed and pondered what would have to be done.

Remedy for the Grumble-Flies

Of course, there was an antidote – a very good remedy – for Grumble-Flies. It was in a book in the vast library in the Judges' Academy. The book was entitled 'Uses for the Oil of Gladness'. The Oil of Gladness was helpful for many ailments that arose from grumbling, complaining, griping and so on. For dealing with the Grumble-Flies, this is what it said:

'The following method is recommended to produce Oil of Gladness (Psalm 45:7) for the eradication of a colony of Grumble-Flies:

> ➢ *Using a bottle or similar vessel for containment, quote Bible passages and verses of Praise, and Psalms of*

Praise (for example, Psalms 146, 147, 148, 149, 150);

➢ *Add to these Praises Prayers of Thanksgiving (for example, Psalm 105:1, 106:1, 118:1, 136);*

➢ *Deliver the bottle containing Thanksgiving and Praise to the Room of Precious Ointments at the Prayer Academy;*

➢ *At the Room of Precious Ointments, the bottle should be filled to the top with the pure Water of Sound Doctrine – equivalent in portion to the Prayers and Praises;*

➢ *The resulting Oil of Gladness ointment should glow bright golden in the container;*

➢ *Once the Oil of Gladness is complete, spray it directly onto the colony of Grumble-Flies; the flies should immediately dissolve;*

➢ *Clean away any remaining Grumble-Fly residue with pure Water of Sound Doctrine;*

➢ *Do all with thanksgiving and without complaint.*

The key to dealing with the Grumble-Flies was praise and thanksgiving based on the teaching of the Bible. Grumble-Flies could not survive when people began to think about and talk about the incredible things that God had done for them, and to thank and praise Him for their great salvation. There were so many wonderful verses from the Bible that would dispel the Grumble-Flies. They would drop down dead and dissolve entirely away under Bible-based praise and thanksgiving, watered with the Water of Sound Doctrine, which was the whole Truth of the Bible.

The problem was the scale of the infestation. It had happened gradually: people had become so disheartened and complaining that the Grumble-Flies had multiplied without anyone realising. By now, a massive quantity of Oil of Gladness was needed to eradicate all the Grumble-Flies from Aletheia – from all the plants and vegetation; from the roofs, walls and foundations of buildings; from thousands of nests and colonies underground. How could they produce such vast quantities of Oil of Gladness when so many people were still complaining? The leaders of Aletheia formed a plan. The plan involved every willing, uncomplaining person, even the students of Aletheia:

This was the project that Gamrie was so interested in.

Gamrie gets to work

As was often the case, Gamrie's dreams of deeds of great, heroic glory were not going to come true. He imagined himself single-handedly tackling vast nests of Grumble-Flies. It seemed so easy. Say the right words from the Bible, bottle them up with Water of Sound Doctrine, and whole, horrible swarms of the tiny, pesky creatures would simply evaporate. What the adults were worried about was beyond him, but he was glad he was able to be involved. Besides, it would all count towards his permanently joining the Academy of Soldiers-of-the-Cross one day.

The task of the volunteer students was not as glorious as Gamrie dreamed, but it *was* important. The people of Aletheia must pray, and praise, and bottle all the thanksgiving they possibly could. Through that long, continually wet summer, the volunteer students would go door-to-door through Aletheia, collecting bottled praise and carrying it carefully to the Precious Ointments' Room in the Prayer Academy. There were strict rules for their work – they simply couldn't afford to break or lose one genuine bottle of thanksgiving. All were needed in the fight against the Grumble-Flies. The students must carefully handle the containers and record what was collected. They were given small hand-carts – a bit like flat-topped wheelbarrows. The bottles were stored in a specially made rack on top. There were explicit instructions about not pushing it too fast, and certainly no one was allowed to ride on it, otherwise you can be sure Gamrie would have been the first to try.

By now, there were so many Grumble-Flies that the walls of some houses were alive with angry buzzing, especially on The Outskirts. Where people prayed they didn't multiply so quickly, but there were still plenty of unhappy people to feed the flies with their complaints.

As the summer progressed, as the leaders of Aletheia desperately tried to encourage people to turn to thankfulness instead of grumbling, it was a pretty *thankless* task trudging about the streets of Aletheia collecting bottled praise. The folk on The Outskirts of Aletheia generated little thankfulness; there were next to no bottles to collect from there. So the volunteers worked their way systematically around the streets of Aletheia, and across the Pray-Always Farmlands. Plenty of the student volunteers dropped out. The ones that remained were very busy indeed.

Gamrie proves his worth

It was not in Gamrie's nature to grumble, and he proved it very well that summer. Day after day, from early in the morning to late at night, he worked around the streets of Aletheia, collecting bottles, recording them diligently on the chart, stowing them carefully on the cart, delivering them to the appointed back door of the Prayer Academy – to go to the Precious Ointments' Room. It was nothing to Gamrie how wet, or dirty, or cold he got. The rain continued to fall and Gamrie became a familiar sight around the city – stopping at doors and collecting small offerings of praise in all sorts of bottles and containers.

Summer flowers drooped unhappily. The streets ran with rivulets of water. People began to burn winter fuel and stay indoors. It was perhaps even worse on the Pray-Always Farmlands, but Gamrie was always the first to volunteer to collect bottles from there. Squelching across soaked fields was a delight to him. The folk on the farmlands, the farmers who had always thought his offers of assistance more hazardous than helpful, now greeted him warmly. He was always invited in, and fed scones and cake and hot chocolate and just about anything else he wanted, as a reward for his efforts in coming so far.

He always enjoyed calling on Aunt Tess and Uncle Thatch where they lived on their farm. Thatch always had bottles and other containers of thanksgiving for Gamrie to collect. Gamrie suspected there wasn't a single Grumble-Fly settled on the Croft farmstead: they were far too thankful to grumble.

Gamrie even produced his own bottles. He memorised Bible passages about thankfulness, and prayed and praised as he walked the streets. His favourite verse was '*Thanks be to God for His indescribable gift!*' because it was a verse about the Lord Jesus and the fact that He was the best, the only, gift that God could give to save the world.

The biggest container

One particularly wet and stormy day, Gamrie reported for work as usual – to a small back door of the Academy of Soldiers-of-the-Cross. He never got far inside the Academy, which he was sorry about, but he still felt as if he was a real Rescuer reporting for duty and involved in the work. A sergeant was stationed at the door with lists of bottle collections due that day. Volunteers were dispatched according to their ability to collect them.

Very few were available for duty that day. The weather was simply too wild for people to venture out. Gamrie didn't usually pay much attention to the chatter around him unless he initiated it, but suddenly he overheard Sergeant Methodic say, "We're short of help today, and no mistake. And the expected offering from the Faithful shop is at last ready to collect. The chief had great hopes…"

As quickly as Gamrie had tuned into the conversation, he tuned out. But the words lodged at the back of his mind, and, when he had completed his list for the day and was walking homewards past the Fruit-of-the-Spirit shopping parade… suddenly he remembered.

The Faithful shop! There was an important collection here! And there was no one else to collect it! Well, there was no reason he couldn't do it, experienced as he now was. Why, only the other day Sergeant Methodic had commented that he was their most faithful collector. How pleased the chief and all the other important managers of Aletheia would be if this special collection was completed today after all!

Gamrie did not suffer from indecisiveness. No sooner had his rapidly moving thoughts come to this conclusion than he abruptly made for the Faithful shop.

It was closing time for most shops in the Fruit-of-the-Spirit shopping parade, but young Mrs De Voté was always the last to shut her small shop. A gust of wind blew furiously down the street and propelled Gamrie to the door. The bell tinkled cheerfully as he entered. Adorning the walls of the shop, folded on neat racks, and hanging on tidy coat hangers, were knitted blankets, hats, gloves, scarves, socks, toys – you name it, the item was knitted in even, brightly coloured stitches and available in the Faithful shop. There was also, rather oddly, something that looked like a covered bathtub, but, to Gamrie's disappointment, the plate of cakes Mrs De Voté often had available for customers had been put away. Mrs De Voté was sweeping the floor, her final task of the day. She stopped abruptly when Gamrie entered.

"And what can I do for you... Gamrie Tickle, isn't it?" she asked, leaning on her brush.

"Yes, ma'am, that's me, ma'am," said Gamrie. "I've come about the bottle collection."

"The bottle...? I see... But it's far more than a bottle-sized container!"

Gamrie nodded as if he knew what she was talking about. "I'm very experienced at bottle collecting now," he said earnestly. "And there was no one else to come... I 'spect on account of the storm..." He gestured dismissively to the howl of wind that at that moment threw large splatters of rain against the window.

Mrs De Voté's twinkling eyes were thoughtful. "Yes, I see, I see..."

"And I've got my cart all ready outside..."

"Indeed..."

Mrs De Voté didn't reveal what she was thinking to Gamrie. She knew that what he had come to collect was precious. She wondered about entrusting this boy with it at all. But who else had ventured out in the storm on this errand? Such efforts deserved rewarding...

She pointed at the bathtub-type container that seemed so out of place in the shop of bright knitting. She asked simply,

"Do you think you can manage it?"

Gamrie scrutinised the excessively bulky container. "That's the biggest one I've ever collected," he said.

"My friends and I have been meeting together all summer," explained Mrs De Voté. "It's the accumulation of a great deal of prayer and thanksgiving and praise."

"Some 'cumulation alright," agreed Gamrie. "You should win a prize!"

Mrs De Voté only smiled. "Now you be careful with this…" She helped Gamrie carry the massive container to the small cart. Although the vessel was large, it was very light, and the wind tried to pull it from them. Of course, it didn't fit on Gamrie's cart properly: it was far too big for that. They balanced it carefully on top. The rain splattered on it. The wind made it sway dangerously.

Mrs De Voté suggested, "Perhaps we should tie it on with a rope? Wait a moment…"

Ever optimistic, Gamrie wasn't sure it needed any anchor at all. But when Mrs De Voté supplied a thick knitted rope, he gamely tied it around the container and the handcart.

The wind and rain whipped around Mrs De Voté, but she didn't seem to notice. She watched her rope being tied securely around the precious prayer-offering. "Now, I don't think any harm can come to it," she said cheerfully.

It was a strange assessment – given the driving rain, the unpredictable gusts of wind, the inadequate handcart, and the inexperienced youth.

Gamrie had no doubts either. He called, "Promise I'll be careful!" and set off.

Precious waste

Threaded through all the roads and thoroughfares of Aletheia were channels of Water of Sound Doctrine. They trickled through carved indentations in the paved streets and kept everything spotlessly clean. It was still raining, and the wind had not abated, when Gamrie left the Faithful shop. He knew all the streets of Aletheia very well by now and contemplated which shortcut he could take to the Prayer Academy to deliver this latest praise offering. The Prayer Academy wasn't far from the Fruit-of-the-Spirit shopping parade, and thankfully it was downhill too. He cut quickly through one street and into another, bumping across the channels of Water of Sound Doctrine, almost colliding with a streetlight at the corner. He was surprised how quickly the small handcart began to move...

The street he found himself on was straight and narrow and all downward. He began to gather speed. Fierce gusts of wind at his back propelled him along even more rapidly until he was going very fast indeed. The precious cargo was not intended to balance at speed on the small handcart: it began to wobble furiously, and Gamrie let go of the hand cart and instead tried to hold onto the ungainly tub. The whole trundling, speeding mass – cart, boy, and cargo – was now completely out of control. When they hit a larger channel of water there was only going to be one outcome. I think you can imagine what happened next…

The cart stopped dead – stuck fast in the channel of Water of Sound Doctrine. Gamrie went flying head over heels. The massive container flew through the air and landed with a sickening crunch in the street. The knitted rope came loose. Through the air it moved like an elegant kite, coming to land gently over Gamrie himself.

From his sprawled position on the rain drenched street, Gamrie watched, horrified as the container split open – smashed and useless. Small tendrils of something like steam sneaked out of the broken vessel and escaped into the air. The precious container of praise and thanksgiving, that might have been vital to rid Aletheia of the Grumble-Flies, was utterly wasted.

Gold

As Gamrie got slowly to his feet, a shout from behind him made his misery all the worse. Sergeant Methodic, having tried, and failed, to collect the cargo from the Faithful shop, had set off in pursuit of Gamrie, fearing exactly what he now perceived had happened. In silence, the sergeant and Gamrie surveyed the mess.

Sergeant Methodic at last demanded, "What have you got to say for yourself?"

For once, Gamrie had nothing to say. Which is precisely what he said. "Nothin', sir."

The rain began to abate. Even the wind, having done its mischief, at last ran out of fury.

The sergeant looked more compassionately on the crestfallen boy. He knew how hard he, of all the students, had worked that summer. "We'll talk about it another time," he said more gently. "For now, we must..."

Suddenly Gamrie grasped the sergeant's arm. "Sir! Oh, look, sir!"

The broken container lay near another small channel of the Water of Sound Doctrine. In the glitter of that water, there was a hint of *gold*.

Eagerly, both man and boy stepped over the broken pieces and peered into the small channel. As they watched, the colour of gold in the water deepened, and glowed, and shimmered, increasing rapidly moment by moment, as though a living thing. Methodic ran to the next channel, and the next, followed at every step by Gamrie. They were *all* turning to gold!

Up the street, around a corner, into Redemption Square rushed the sergeant. Gamrie was forgotten, but he followed anyway. What a wonderful, incredible sight! The channels of water, which threaded hither and thither across Redemption Square to the cross, were the purest gold. Far faster than they could run, all the rivulets of Water of Sound Doctrine were turning to gold. They were dancing, swirling, bubbling, gurgling; they emitted glittering, gold-tinted steam; and when the rain abruptly ceased, and the sun just as suddenly shone, the 'steam' turned to all the colours of the rainbow.

The people of Aletheia began to come outside when the sun shone. They stepped from their homes all over the city, amazed that the rain had stopped and that the sun was shining again. They noticed with far greater astonishment the channels of golden water on their streets. Farther and farther the mass of self-mixed Oil of Gladness penetrated the linked waterways of the city, and all across the Pray-Always Farmlands, until, at last, it reached the boundary of Aletheia.

As the clouds fled in fright from the stormy sky, as the wind hid its face in shame and died away altogether, the whole city was surrounded by shimmering gold.

What happened to the Grumble-Flies?

You can probably imagine what happened to the Grumble-Flies once the entire air of Aletheia was permeated with the Oil of Gladness. In hundreds and thousands and millions they dissolved entirely. In bushes and trees and walls and roofs and houses, nests and colonies of Grumble-Flies evaporated under the fragrance of thanksgiving. Of course, in some houses there would always be a few living and thriving. Where people grumbled, the pesky creatures would always survive. But the epidemic of them was gone and people learned to be thankful to God again.

The leaders, and people, of Aletheia were greatly relieved at this previously undiscovered remedy for an epidemic of Grumble-Flies. When the whole story was known they could still hardly believe the unexpected course of events that led to the cleansing of the city and thankfulness being restored. But for Gamrie's accident, no one would have thought of adding the offering of the prayers of thanksgivings to the aboveground channels of Water of Sound Doctrine. The whole event, and the remedy, was carefully recorded in the Judges' Academy; Gamrie Tickle was even mentioned by name.

The knitted rope

I should add that one further detail, and it's about the knitted rope that Mrs De Voté gave to secure the large tub to Gamrie's cart. Gamrie took it home and stored it away; I think it probably still lies in a forgotten corner in an attic in Aletheia. But Gamrie was unaware of the part it played in turning to good his impulsive action and protecting him from greater disaster. You see, while Mrs De Voté knits, she prays. And the knitted pieces she gives away are pledges that she is praying. Mrs De Voté wasn't quite as surprised as the rest of the city that things turned out the way they did. She had prayed for Gamrie and that precious cargo – that it might be used to eradicate the Grumble-Flies from Aletheia. She knew the great power of prayer.

And, if you've read *The Purple Storm* you'll know that when

Mrs De Voté was an old lady, a knitted prayer pledge also made all the difference in a very dangerous adventure…

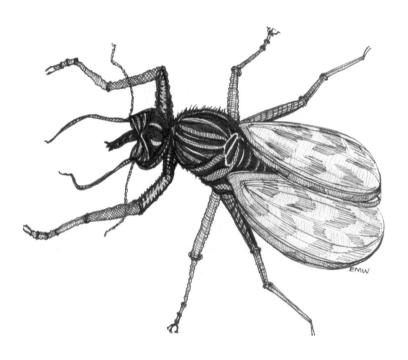

THE GRUMBLE-FLIES

Bible Verses

Ephesians 5:20:

'Giving thanks always for all things to God the Father in the name of our Lord Jesus Christ.'

2 Corinthians 9:15:

'Thanks be to God for His indescribable gift!'

Ephesians 3:20-21:

'Now to Him who is able to do exceedingly abundantly above all that we ask or think, according to the power that works in us, to Him be glory...'

Bible Lesson – Be Thankful!

1. Prayer is a great way to be thankful – and it really does help to stop grumbling. We should take time every day to thank God for His goodness.

2. Like the Grumble-Flies, grumbling can multiply! It's very contagious to other people and often it grows into a habit before we're aware of it. Prayer and gratitude to God is the best way to stop grumbling.

3. Although there were other factors that affected the outcome of Gamrie's accident in this adventure (such as Mrs De Voté's prayers), he was willing and diligent and was able to be used for the good of Aletheia. We ought to be willing, diligent and faithful in God's service. God can use a willing person to achieve wonderful things, far above what we might ask or imagine we can do in His service.

5. SAVING ALETHEIA

Following his unexpected heroism in the eradication of the Grumble-Flies, Gamrie, still a High School student but presumably now more reliable and responsible, was once more allowed to work as a volunteer in his beloved Academy of Soldiers-of-the-Cross. Officer Queenie Staple, who had *not* forgotten him, preferred not to have Gamrie's '*help*' in the General Supplies Department. After some deliberation on the part of managers in the Academy who were familiar with Gamrie's interesting track record, he was placed under the supervision of Mr Ivan Spanner, Maintenance Department Manager in the Academy.

Frankly, Gamrie considered this a promotion from his previous position at the Academy. After all, no matter how much Officer Staple liked correctly counted pencils, mending machines and repairing stuff was surely much more important than *that*.

Actually, the job to which Gamrie was assigned was not the glamorous job he had imagined – taking apart engines, welding metal, repairing and sorting exciting machines. In fact, he was to be allowed very little 'hands on' work at all, no matter how earnestly he put his case to Mr Spanner.

"I can help with the mending an' repairing an' stuff, sir. Honestly, I think I could learn…" he said.

Mr Spanner cleared his throat and Gamrie subsided into respectful silence. The manager clutched what was once a neatly printed, pressed report. It was no longer quite so neat: Mr Spanner's large hands were invariably covered in greasy oil from his work, and he did not much care about paperwork. He spent as little time as possible in his office, leaving the running of it to an efficient secretary. But the paperwork that had accompanied this boy made interesting reading – even to him. The boy didn't *look* like a trouble-maker. If anything, he appeared to be on the verge of laughter, as if the world around him was about to reveal a good joke. But he looked strong enough to lift and move and carry: and that was all he would be entrusted with for the time being.

"You'll be working with Jaw Wrench, head of our team who carry out Repairs Assessments," said Mr Spanner. "Jaw works throughout the Academy, attending any jobs that come in – whether emergency repairs or routine maintenance. He – or one of his team – assesses the job and decides who should do it and when it should be done. He always carries his bag of tools and other equipment with him, so you will be there to fetch and carry whatever he wants. Are you clear?"

The young man grinned. "Yes, sir, of course, sir! There's nothing much to remember about all of that, is there?" Earnestly he added, "I'll do everything Mr Wrench says. I won't do anything wrong. No more accidents for me, oh no, sir!" His cheerful reference to the so-called *accident* in the past took Mr Spanner somewhat by surprise. There was no one in the vast Academy who had not heard of the serious incident in the Vomitorium a couple of years before. His own Maintenance Department had been rushed off their feet helping with the clean-up. It was one of the most costly 'accidents' the Academy had ever seen. But this, it seemed, had passed Gamrie Tickle by.

Mr Spanner took a moment to reiterate Gamrie's place in the scheme of things. "You will not interfere with, touch, move, or handle anything you're not asked to, Tickle. No more accidents, do you understand?"

The look on Gamrie's face was curious: a mix of hurt and bewilderment. "I don't see how I can help an *accident*, sir," he said. "After all, accidents just happen, don't they?"

Mr Spanner watched the boy leave. He was likeable enough, and certainly willing. If he was watched closely, what harm could he do...?

The odd trio

Jaw Wrench was a tall, paper-thin, sinewy man, built rather like a pipe, except that he could bend. He was also a taciturn man, and had preferred the days when he was a less prominent member of the Maintenance Department. He enjoyed appearing silently at a job and spending the day mending and sorting and restoring whatever it was that needed attention. In those days he was seldom required to speak to anyone at all.

But since his skill and seniority had promoted him to head up the Repairs Assessments, his quiet world had disintegrated. He still said as little as possible, so every word was sure to count. Those who knew him best listened carefully; those who didn't missed the point.

When Jaw Wrench was promoted, the supervisor, Mr Spanner, gave him an assistant – a young man called Sim Ratchet. Sim loved his job. He learnt the name of all the tools; took pride in organising them; and whatever he lacked in academic ability, he made up for in willingness to work. He trotted contentedly after Mr Wrench all over the Academy; and he seldom required an answer from his mostly silent boss. So the two of them – quiet Jaw Wrench and his young assistant – managed quite well.

It was with some misgivings that Mr Wrench heard of the appointment of another helper. Unlike Mr Spanner, he did not recollect the name of Gamrie Tickle, nor did he associate him with the well-known disaster at the Vomitorium. Jaw simply wished they would leave him and Sim and their work alone. But Jaw did not question or protest at the company of another assistant. And so, Gamrie joined them.

Sim Ratchet and Gamrie Tickle hit it off straightaway. Sim was extremely glad of the company, and in Gamrie he found a friend nearer his age who also liked the tools and equipment they were tasked to carry around. On the other hand, Gamrie found in Sim a companion who appreciated his jokes and liked his suggestions. Gamrie was far cleverer than Sim (although this was not always apparent) and it was not difficult to kid Sim and play the odd practical joke; Sim always fell for it hook, line, and sinker; and Sim always laughed.

As the days turned into weeks, this odd trio could be seen here and there about the Academy – the tall, thin man trailed by two teenagers carrying his equipment and chattering between themselves. Mr Spanner stopped worrying about Gamrie Tickle. There were no *serious* mishaps that came to his attention (if you ignored the number of tools that were mislaid or left behind when the boys were distracted, the broken window when Gamrie threw a hammer for Sim to catch, and a couple of other breakages that were never reported). From what Mr Spanner could gather from Jaw Wrench, he was satisfied enough with the arrangement, and had even been spotted laughing quietly at one of Gamrie's jokes. And so the days passed.

The Stair-Gobbler

Do you have stairs in your house? Whatever they're like, and however many there are, I don't suppose they're anything like the massive winding staircase at the centre of the Academy of Soldiers-of-the-Cross. It was a *gigantic* staircase. It wound round and round the thick walls of the castle, again and again and again, moving from one floor to the next until it became a mere speck high up in the far distance of the highest turret of the huge Academy, or disappeared into the deepest, darkest depths of the foundations below.

There were two parts to the stairs. There was the pedestrian part – where people could walk from one floor to the next along the outside rail of the staircase, much as you would in our world. And there were slender, almost invisible, rails along the inside of the staircase – reserved solely for the fantastic Stair-Gobbler. At each floor the Stair-Gobbler – or people – could stop. There was a platform for the Gobbler and steps for pedestrians. It was carefully designed so that people didn't get run over.

It was no surprise that this staircase, and the Stair-Gobbler, was of immense interest to both Gamrie and Sim. If you had ever seen the Stair-Gobbler fly across the rails, taking busy Rescuers and other staff from one location of the enormous Academy to another, you would understand why Sim and Gamrie were fascinated. It was called a 'Gobbler' because it appeared to gobble up the stairs. In reality, the long, slender, rounded capsule flew smoothly across the rails, lightning-fast, breathtakingly-swift, stomach-churning and crazy – but it was the desire of every adventurous person to ride in it.

It was not granted to Gamrie or Sim to do this. In fact, it was strictly forbidden. While the controls of the Gobbler were surprisingly simple, it was only Rescuers of a certain rank who were trusted to convey people in it. It was still a relatively new invention; those who knew the most about it were never sure what unexpected things might happen under the interference of those who didn't know what they were doing. It was simply too new and too unpredictable.

Gamrie and Sim were probably the only people in the whole of the busy Academy who were delighted when the Stair-Gobbler broke down. This was the closest they were likely to get to it and they happily followed Mr Wrench to inspect the machine and see what might be required to mend it.

On arrival, they saw nothing more auspicious than the light, slender capsule sitting quietly at the landing station of Floor 12, close to their own department. Nearby stood a young Rescuer. She said respectfully to Mr Wrench, "I was watching it until you came, sir. Just to see that no one tried to use it until you had a chance to inspect it. It shuddered to a stop with a sort of *crunch*, so Captain Steadfast wanted it checked before it's back in use."

Mr Wrench nodded in agreement and the Rescuer disappeared. Gamrie and Sim followed their boss to the capsule, watching closely as he inspected the controls. There was no dazzling array of buttons and dials. There was a lever attached to a circle – a bit like a driving wheel with a handle sticking out of the side. Around the edge of the circle were numerous destinations within the Academy. You simply pulled the lever round and round until it pointed where you wanted to go. Currently it was set to 'Slides'. There was a big, green button labelled 'Go'. The Gobbler was programmed to stop wherever you set the lever, but there was, in addition, a red button offset to the side that was labelled 'Emergency Stop', and one other button – coloured yellow – that was labelled 'Override'.

Mr Wrench carefully inspected the Gobbler's runners. "Spanner, runner-claw, 13.9," he said quietly.

Gamrie handed the heavy tool bag to Sim as he had done many times before. Sim opened the tool bag and prepared to remove the runner-claw spanner 13.9 that had its own particular place with the other runner-claws. Sim was very orderly about such things.

"Oh…" Sim peered deeper into the bag with a frown. "Uh, it's not here, sir. Sorry, sir, but I think we must have left it at that job yesterday, remember when you used it…"

Mr Wrench straightened up and sighed. He could see that one of the Gobbler's runners had caught on a small nail. It wasn't much, but it was enough to bring the finely-tuned machine to a crunching stop. It might be as simple as removing the nail and checking that the runner was smooth before the busy Gobbler was back in use. Then he and the boys could continue their part of the annual inspection of the Academy's 760 windows. Their team only had 171 to go…

Sim's head hung low with shame. He took his job seriously. "Sorry, sir," he said again.

Mr Wrench nodded. "There's one in the department I can use," he said. He paused. Neither of the two boys would know where the spanner was; it was a five-minute job for him to go and retrieve it.

Gamrie said eagerly, "We'll guard the Stair-Gobbler, sir. We won't let anyone near it until you get back!"

With unusual firmness, Mr Wrench said, "Do *not* touch

anything."

"No, sir," said Sim.

"No, sir, of course not, sir!" added Gamrie.

"Five minutes," said Mr Wrench in parting, and then his tall, spare figure was striding quickly along the passageway back to the maintenance workshop to fetch the spare runner-claw spanner 13.9.

It was enough for both boys to stand guard by the Stair-Gobbler. Arms folded, feeling important, they blocked the way, explaining to the folk trudging up and down the stairs that it was 'officially' out of use until it was mended. They enjoyed using the word *officially*.

Gamrie said, "We're the *official* guardians of the Stair-Gobbler."

Sim nodded sober agreement. While they were in charge, *no one* would get by.

Interpreting the rules

After what felt like a long time, but was in fact about two minutes, Gamrie said, "We could sit in it. You know, just guard it while we sit in it."

Sim asked doubtfully, "Isn't that touching it?"

"Well, it's not *exactly* touching it in the way that Mr Wrench meant. He meant not pressing buttons and stuff. But if we *sat* in it, all the Rescuers who want to use it would see that they can't get in. In fact, it might even be *safer* that way!"

Sim brightened. The way Gamrie presented it, Mr Wrench had positively intended that they should be sitting in the Stair-Gobbler. They might even be neglecting their duty by waiting outside! First Gamrie, then Sim, entered the double front seat of the low-lying open capsule. The rounded see-through cover, which clamped down for safety when the Gobbler was in use, remained open. Nothing happened. Gamrie put on his seat-belt. It was nice to pretend that they could go for a ride, even if they couldn't.

At that moment, a young trainee, Sapphire Happenstance, arrived on the scene. In her hand she clutched a bulging folder. She immediately climbed into the seat behind the two boys. She was out of breath from running down several flights of stairs. She was evidently in a great hurry.

"Quickly, please! I must get this report to Lieutenant Duffle himself! It's *vitally* important!"

Sim swung around to stare at the girl wearing the smart trainee's uniform. She looked impressive; far more important than he thought he was. "We can't... it's not... we're not..."

"Quick! You must! Every moment counts!"

Gamrie pondered. Was the urgent file for Lieutenant Duffle more important than not using the Stair-Gobbler? What if the file contained something about the destruction of the entire city of Aletheia? Mr Wrench had commented that the Gobbler seemed OK and would be easily mended...

Sim continued to protest. He saw everything in shades of black or white and was not prone to explore grey areas or wonder at hidden shades of meaning in instructions. Mr Wrench had said 'don't touch': so they should not touch that big green button, no matter how attractive and persistent this distressed trainee was.

Gamrie, however, liked to examine possibilities – whether real or imagined. If there was any chance of a devastating attack on the Academy, which might be stopped by the small risk of taking the nice young recruit on a Gobbler ride to see the lieutenant, surely it was nothing less than their duty.

Sim was protesting, "We can't even drive it!"

"Just press *GO!*" cried the exasperated girl. "I've seen it done dozens of times! Can't you even do that much?"

"No," said Sim stubbornly. "We were told not to touch. We're only maintenance, you know, to fix things…"

Gamrie was still deliberating whether the entire fate of Aletheia was in his hands. Ought he to save his city, and please this impressive girl, by simply pressing the 'Go' button?

The instant he decided that it was up to him to play the part of heroic rescuer, Sapphire also came to a decision. As Gamrie reached for the button, swiftly, suddenly, Sapphire leaned forward and also jabbed hard at the green 'Go'.

A wild ride

Before any of them had time to draw another breath, the Stair-Gobbler shot like a rocket from its station and catapulted itself at breakneck speed down the winding staircase. A horrified shout – the loudest ever heard from the approaching Mr Wrench – was lost as the wind rang in their ears, blocking everything else out.

In the first few seconds, the safety roof, which had failed to close, began to break free. Sim wasn't even belted in. He clutched anything he possibly could – grasping wildly around and managing to grab hold of Gamrie. As for Sapphire, an unearthly scream rang out and, in the first few seconds, she vanished from the Gobbler.

The two friends didn't stop. Round and down at impossible speed they flew. They had no words – their shouts were lost in the loud wail of the wind in their ears. They could do nothing but hang on and wait for it to stop.

Somewhere in the darkness of underground Aletheia it did exactly that. With an unhealthy crunch, the Gobbler came to an abrupt halt and catapulted both boys –Gamrie with his seatbelt wrapped around him – onto...

...a very soft landing! In fact, onto something like a cross between a trampoline and a massive mattress!

True to its original destination, the Gobbler had taken them to a Slide-Landing.

When they stopped bouncing on the soft landing and found their shaky legs again, Sim stared around in utter bewilderment.

"Wh-wh-where a-are we?" he stammered.

They were clearly deep underground, and the landing place by which they had stopped had the peculiar look of an old-fashioned railway station. Sim and Gamrie wouldn't have called it this – they weren't familiar with old train stations. But if you had been there you might have thought of this. There were slender rails – like elegant train tracks – for the Stair-Gobbler. A raised platform at the side of the rails (where Gamrie and Sim had just landed) was made of bouncy foam. Picturesque, antiquated street lights cast a glow over the 'station' – the type you might see on old-fashioned Christmas cards, except these were lit by a brightly-shining Bible. The thick walls of the station building went straight up through the high stone ceiling. And, most reassuringly of all, there was a tall, uniformed man sweeping the 'platform' – except that he had just dropped his broom in astonishment. The man wore a badge on his uniform. It stated, 'Mr Hearty Wallop, Slide-Landings Keeper'.

Gamrie tried his best to regain his balance even while his head still spun round and round from their wild ride. "Are we in underground Aletheia, sir?" he asked.

"I should think you are, young man," retorted Hearty Wallop. He picked up his brush and pointed with it at the forlorn-looking Stair-Gobbler. "Now, explain what you were doing on *that*!" From his stern tone it was obvious that he already knew they were there without permission.

Gamrie sighed. "It was broken," he said, somewhat irrelevantly.

Sim looked decidedly sick from the ride. "We were t-told not to t-touch it," he said.

Through the more detailed explanation that followed, Mr Wallop was *not* favourably impressed with their account, no matter how much Gamrie was convinced their course of action was the only reasonable one under the circumstances. Hearty Wallop contacted Lieutenant Duffle himself via the link in his small 'station' office, and shortly thereafter the lieutenant entered Mr Wallop's office in person.

When Gamrie was asked what led to his decision to drive the Gobbler, he said, "I was only trying to save Aletheia!"

More about Slides and other details

I'd love to tell you more about the Slide-Landings and other secret Slides of Aletheia, but this book is about Gamrie Tickle. If you read *The Defenders of Aletheia* you'll learn some more about them there. You might also have wondered how it was that Lieutenant Duffle managed to reach Hearty Wallop's office so quickly – especially since he didn't have use of the Stair-Gobbler. Gamrie never did discover how, but actually, the Lieutenant took one of the secret Slides reserved for important people in the Academy. But they must wait for another story.

In case you're wondering what happened to Sapphire Happenstance, I should explain that once she had been ejected from the Stair-Gobbler she took no further part in any adventure for quite some time. She spent the next few weeks in the hospital wing of the Academy with a broken leg, dislocated shoulder, and a stiff reprimand. The contents of the important folder she had with her were scattered across every floor of the Academy. Just in case you're also wondering – the city of Aletheia was not destroyed because of the loss, but the contents of the folder *were* extremely important… but that must also wait for another story.

SAVING ALETHEIA
Bible Verses
John 14:15: 'If you love Me, keep My commandments.'   **Acts 5:29**: 'We ought to obey God...'
Bible Lesson – Be Obedient!

1. In this story, Gamrie got completely carried away interpreting the rules he had been given according to what he wanted to do – and, as you know, it led to disaster! We must beware of interpreting what God wants us to do according to what we want to do. It's easy to convince ourselves that what we want to do is fine with God too.

2. As Christians, we ought always to take our instructions from the Word of God, the Bible, and obey God through keeping in line with the teaching of the Bible. In this way, we can show our love to the Lord Jesus – by obeying His commands.

3. Good Bible teachers and godly older Christians can help us ensure that we understand the teaching of the Bible and don't get too carried away with our own ideas and interpretation of God's will for our lives.

6. LET IT SNOW!

Does it snow at Christmastime where you live? In Aletheia everyone wanted snow at Christmas. This particular winter something very curious happened – and it was all about snow. I'm sure you've already guessed that Gamrie Tickle was in the middle of it.

A few years have gone by and Gamrie has now left school and at last begun his formal training at the Academy of Soldiers-of-the-Cross. Plenty of people thought it would never happen: especially after the incident in the Vomitorium and with the Stair-Gobbler. But others remembered about his part in eradicating the plague of Grumble-Flies, and the way he had been so faithful in helping all through that difficult summer. So it was decided he should be allowed a place to start his training. Gamrie's dream had finally come true; he was learning how to be a Rescuer.

At the beginning of their training, the young recruits worked their way around all of the departments in the Academy of Soldiers-of-the-Cross. This meant that they could learn about the various jobs and roles that were available. Gamrie enjoyed every moment.

The Central Control Room

The Central Control Room was vitally important in the work of the Academy. Quite simply, it was the place which controlled pretty much everything. It was a massive round chamber with a circular viewing balcony – the Observer Deck – high above the room. If you stood on this platform, you would look down on the most fascinating machines, instruments, devices, and other things that you could ever imagine. The machines tracked every Rescuer in the land of Err; showed how much prayer power was generated and how safe this made Aletheia; recorded every prayer request for help from people in the land of Err; tracked storms; showed weather patterns and predictions; alerted Aletheia to sudden, imminent danger, and so on and on. There were so many complicated devices – whirring, bubbling, clanking, clicking, buzzing, spinning, flashing. There were so many lights, buttons, needles, dials, colours… it was a blur of coordinated activity: and Professor Nea Stigmine was in charge of it all.

Professor Stigmine was the youngest manager ever appointed to the Central Control Room. She was a brilliant scientist – possibly the best the Academy had ever seen. She met Gamrie when he joined them for two weeks of initiation training in December. The Professor read his file with interest, even amusement, and on his arrival summoned him to her office.

"So, you're Trainee Gamrie Tickle," she said.

Gamrie scanned the petite lady behind the impressive desk. "Yes, ma'am," he returned politely.

"You've got quite an interesting record, young man."

"Thank you, ma'am."

"Would you say you were prone to accident or trouble, Tickle?"

Gamrie considered the questioned seriously. "No, ma'am," he said. "Although, sometimes interestin' things have happened."

"Have they indeed?" She sounded amused. "Certainly your file suggests that trouble knows where to find you."

"Does it, ma'am?"

"It does, Trainee, and I'm afraid I won't allow your friend, Trouble, into the Control Room!"

"No, ma'am. Of course not, ma'am." Gamrie struggled to follow why she thought Trouble was a real person who might be his friend, but he didn't think he should ask. Maybe she got confused because she was so scientific and clever.

"There are certain rules you will obey at all times, in every situation."

"Yes, ma'am."

"Under no circumstances will you touch or handle anything unless you are explicitly instructed to do so."

"Of course not, ma'am."

She thought his answer was ambiguous. "You mean, of course, that you won't touch or handle anything unless you're told to do so?"

"Of course, ma'am."

"You understand what this means?"

"Yes, ma'am."

"So, if you're working with my team on, let's say, the Storm Tracker, and you're asked to request a forecast of a storm connected to the latest Meddler activity in the land of Err, what will you do?"

"Whatever they say, ma'am," said Gamrie promptly, thinking that this was abundantly obvious.

"And if you're left on your own at the machine, and there's a fire in the building, what will you do?"

"Nothin', ma'am," said Gamrie, certain this was by far the safest answer. He knew a good joke about fires, but he thought it best not to mention it.

"Perhaps that's not the best example," muttered the Professor, not convinced that the young man knew what she was talking about. "The point is, Tickle, that you will *not*, even in extreme circumstances, interfere with any machine in the Control Room!"

Gamrie began to wonder if the Professor was as clever as everyone said. This stuff was obvious. "Of course not, ma'am."

Professor Stigmine sighed. She still wasn't certain she had adequately made the point and she was all too aware that even the slightest interference with some of the fantastic machines could yield quite startling, not to say disruptive and extremely destructive, results. "You will be under the supervision of one of our machine managers, Boff Buffer," said the Professor.

"Thank you, ma'am."

She watched Trainee Tickle walk away. He was only with them for two weeks until the Christmas holidays. Surely nothing much could happen in that time…

The Weather Guide Machine

Gamrie's favourite machine in the Control Room was the Weather Guide. There were so many appealing things about it. To begin with, it looked pretty impressive – a large, glass globe, balanced between rounded, shining brass arms. The brass arms had spiky fingers sticking out at all angles – which were finely-tuned receivers of weather data. At the base there was a screen. You could write with your finger across the screen, and press controls to give you readings about all sorts of weather across the entire land of Err. As you know, the weather often indicated what people were doing in Err, and this machine would record, track, monitor and even predict what was likely to be coming.

But possibly the best thing about it was that whatever you were searching for appeared in the large, see-through globe. When Gamrie first learned this he was so eager to see a demonstration that Boff Buffer allowed the Weather Guide team to satisfy Gamrie's curiosity. Mrs Ćlimăté Ćontrollĕr, a cheerful, outdoorsy lady with a weather-beaten face, carefully input Gamrie's request – '*Weather in the Mountains of Destruction?*' – into the machine. Sure enough, in the wonderful crystal-clear globe, the faint outline of the frightful Mountains of Destruction in the north of the land of Err took shape, drawn by an invisible hand. Water began to gush down the crooked gullies of the mountains. Crevasses filled with snow. Dark clouds formed above the mountain range and real snow actually began to fall inside the globe, covering the mountains with a fresh coating of white.

Gamrie was entranced. He requested the snow conditions in the towns of Topsy-Turvy and Make-Believe. It was so extraordinary to watch the snow in these strange places that Gamrie was inspired to make up new jokes about snow – until Mrs Ćlimăté Ćontrollĕr, afraid the new trainee wasn't taking the Weather Guide seriously enough, declined any further requests.

"Just one more, ma'am," said Gamrie. "For my younger sister. You see, she always wants snow at Christmas, and if you could just…"

Ćlimăté good-naturedly entered this final question into the Weather Guide machine. *'Christmas forecast for Aletheia?'* In actual fact, she already knew the answer because she had already checked. It wasn't for herself (or so she said); it was because wherever she went in December in Aletheia that was the one question all her friends were sure to ask.

To Gamrie's dismay, above the outline of Aletheia the globe filled with light clouds and soft, filtered sunshine. The glitter of frost was over the city, but it was going to be a green Christmas.

And one thing the wonderful Weather Guide was unable to do, was change the weather.

Weavel Seeds

When Professor Nea Stigmine mentioned the example of a fire in the building she didn't expect anything of the sort to disrupt the important work of the Central Control Room of the Academy. As it happened, it wasn't a fire that emptied the Control Room on Gamrie's final day of initiation training: it was Weavel Seeds.

For several months, the Academy of Soldiers-of-the-Cross had been monitoring a curious development that was taking place in the Academy of Science-Explains-All in the land of Err. This particular development first appeared on the Control Room's radar back in the summer – an innocuous reading on the Trouble Trace machine. The warning was,

'*Low level threat: invasive seed development at ASEA* (meaning the Academy of Science-Explains-All); *potential to contaminate crops.*'

There was always some trouble filtering through from inventions in the land of Err – creatures, robots, devices, and yes, some plant material too. The warning wasn't forgotten, but neither the Trouble Trace nor the Revealer Device showed any significant cause for concern at this development. The Control Room, and other departments at the Academy, simply monitored and waited. Nothing happened until the winter – at the same time as Gamrie was doing his introductory training at the Control Room.

The Academy as a whole, and the Control Room in particular, were taken by surprise when, one frosty morning, Thatch Straw paid an urgent visit – clutching a tightly sealed bag containing a small, round, spiky, most unfriendly-looking pod. It was a Weavel Seed.

How he got the seed is a whole other story, but to summarise the relevant point for our story – this poisonous, insidious seed had the potential to contaminate all the crops of Aletheia and much else besides. The seeds had been borne over the boundaries of Aletheia on the wind and quietly settled on the bare, winter fields. In the spring they would take hold and the fast-growing, spiky, penetrating roots would weave their way through every living, growing thing on the Pray-Always Farmlands. Worse still, small fragments of the seed had also attached themselves to anyone who had been on the farmlands – and in the warmth of the important buildings of Aletheia, their roots had started to shoot and snag any object they could.

They had already begun to twist their poisonous way into people's homes and work places. By now it was feared that a few people had unknowingly carried it through the back doors of the Academy. People were only supposed to enter the Academy through the front door – past the Contamination Detector that identified any foreign, unwelcome substance and thus kept the Academy safe from the dangerous pollution and contaminants of Err. But a few folk, people running late or taking shortcuts, used back doors.

Only Water of Sound Doctrine would destroy Weavel Seeds. As quickly as possible, the entire Academy must be decontaminated with the water. It kept Mr Spanner's Maintenance Department, and plenty of other departments, frantically busy. They started late in the evening, working through the entire night, and by the time Gamrie arrived at work the following morning – using a back door because he was running late – they had cleansed half the Academy and had just finished the Control Room itself.

Gamrie had not taken a great deal of notice of the chatter about Weavel Seeds. When he walked into the deserted Control Room he certainly didn't associate its emptiness with the latest concern about seeds. Finding the important room completely unoccupied was a curious sensation. The machines still hummed and chattered quietly among themselves, but, for the moment, Gamrie was entirely alone.

Snow!

Had the Professor been remotely aware of the combination of circumstances that had conspired to place Gamrie Tickle momentarily alone in the Control Room, she would instantly have rushed to the freshly decontaminated room and given him a stern reprimand for not only arriving late (and therefore missing her instructions to leave the Control Room for twenty minutes and monitor the machines remotely), but also for daring to use a back door – which was now strictly forbidden. As it was, for twelve and a half minutes Gamrie was on his own.

Gamrie was not dismayed that he was alone in what was arguably the most important, certainly the most fascinating, room in the Academy. You will have learnt by now that not much dismayed him. He was not even particularly curious as to why everyone was absent – something that was unheard of. He was intrigued, and even pleased, to wander at will among the still clicking and clacking machines. He spent some time enjoying watching ice form in wonderful patterns of intricate beauty on the inside of the Weather Guide globe. It formed, then melted, again and again. It was the equivalent of a winter computer screen-saver for the Weather Guide. It was then he noticed a large pipe snaking through the lone, high window of the room. The pipe was swaying around at head-height, looking like an enormous lost snake. Gamrie was puzzled to think what this new device was, and, his eyes fixed on the intriguing pipe, he stumbled against the globe as he left it.

For a while he was quite content to watch the massive wall panel that was a detailed map of the land of Err. It was the main Mission Detector Screen at the Academy. Coloured dots moved across it – indicating Rescuers and people in need, creatures and dangers, transport and machines, and other things besides. Christmas missions were underway across the land. He could see clusters of Rescuers in towns here and there. He imagined the strange things they were encountering in places such as Make-Believe.

Precisely when he first became aware of the chilly blast behind him he could not have said. Nor could he tell Professor Stigmine when she questioned him about it later. He was so absorbed by the action on the screen that it was some time before he tuned into the fact that the Control Room was suddenly getting extremely cold. Gamrie was pretty sturdy and tough and even then he might not have noticed, or bothered, about the decreasing temperature, but for the sudden flake of white that landed on his hand. He examined it, entranced. It vanished immediately, leaving a slight damp patch behind. But as quickly as it had gone, another came, and then another, and then several more, and dozens upon dozens, and in the time that it's taken you to read this sentence, Gamrie was staring in astonishment at an utterly transformed Control Room.

I think it would be safe to say that no one reading this has ever seen anything quite like the scene that greeted Gamrie Tickle. In the vast Central Control Room, deep inside the massive fortress Academy, there was the most terrific snowstorm you can possibly imagine!

All around the room, settling on all the devices, swirling and tumbling and thoroughly enjoying themselves, were large flakes of snow. Even in the seconds that Gamrie had discovered it, the snowstorm increased rapidly until a ferocious blizzard was suddenly raging all about him. Gamrie was transfixed, not only by the sight, but by the fact that the force of the sudden storm pinned him to his place and obscured even the sight of the nearest machine. All was white, swirling snow.

Gamrie takes action

Although Gamrie often made the wrong choice, and although Trouble, as Professor Stigmine had said, was something of a friend, he had learned from his mistakes. In the early moments of his surprise he realised instinctively that the fascinating Weather Guide must be responsible for the snowstorm. It was the only reasonable conclusion to reach. He had a good sense of direction and, through the increasing blizzard, Gamrie slowly fought his way, step by step, to the Weather Guide. Through the blinding snow, he could dimly see the fractured globe. The root of what appeared to be a plant was twisting its way through the glass and had already opened up several large cracks. Every additional crack intensified the snowstorm. This was definitely the cause of the problem... but what should he do about it?

Dimly, then with increasing clarity, he remembered Professor Stigmine's instructions. Even in the event of a fire – she meant an emergency, of course, and this was definitely *that* – he *must not* touch any device in the Control Room. Through the whiteness he could see the red 'off' button that every machine had somewhere on its anatomy. But he *must not* touch it. He scanned the room, searching for other options.

The door through which the workers usually entered the Control Room was already blocked with a heap of snow. The

Observer Deck – the high balcony that circled around the room – could be accessed by the Leveller, but that was now buried beneath a large snowdrift. Gamrie glanced hopelessly up to the Observer Deck. Through the blinding whiteness of the storm it seemed to him that people were waving at him; but he couldn't clearly discern a single gesture. Through the howl of the blizzard there might even have been voices; but nothing they said could reach him above the shriek of the wind.

Suddenly he remembered the snaking pipe. It seemed to him that it was waving to him in the storm, probably blown on the cold wind. He staggered through the snow and caught firm hold of it. He *was* allowed to touch this. After all, it wasn't a machine in the Control Room, was it? On the end of the pipe he felt a switch. With absolutely nothing left to lose he jabbed at the button as hard as he could.

What the pipe did

What he thought might happen when he pressed that button he wasn't clear about afterwards, no matter how hard the infuriated Professor Stigmine tried to extract details. But whatever he might have expected, I don't suppose he thought the massive pipe would do what it did:

It began to suck snow! Like a ginormous vacuum cleaner, it gobbled and grabbed and shoved into its yawning mouth all the snow that was spilling so furiously from the fractured globe of the Weather Guide.

Quite where the snow was going Gamrie couldn't imagine. But in a few minutes the incredible tube had cleared six inches of snow, demolished snowdrifts as if they were a favourite treat, and was even grabbing wildly at the still swirling, falling whiteness – clearing snowflakes from the air around him! With greater clarity, Gamrie could now see Professor Stigmine and her staff, and… was that Lieutenant Duffle, and… Captain Steadfast himself…? The Leveller was now clear of snow, and senior managers began to descend to the Control Room.

Enquiry

Not for the first time, and certainly not for the last, Gamrie Tickle was questioned by important people from the Academy. We've already observed that Gamrie was not at all clear on precisely what happened and when during the incident, or what he expected to happen when he pressed the button on the end of the giant tube.

"I thought it was a bit like a fire, you see," he explained.

"A fire…?" Captain Steadfast turned to Lieutenant Duffle, who in turn glanced questioningly at Professor Stigmine.

Professor Stigmine sighed. She said, "Not like a fire, Tickle! Not similar at all!"

"Sorry ma'am, but I thought you said I was not to touch the machines, no matter what happened…"

"And yet, you introduced a *Weavel root* into the Weather Guide!" cried the Professor.

Gamrie said, "I didn't know about them Weavel things, ma'am. No one explained about Weavels to me..."

Lieutenant Duffle said, "I think we'd better move on from the fact that you didn't press the 'off' button on the Weather Guide. But you were forbidden to use the back door of the Academy specifically to guard against the introduction of dangerous contamination into the Academy. The Control Room had just been cleansed, but because of your lateness, and carelessness using the wrong door – not to say disobedience – you introduced a foreign substance into the heart of the Control Room."

"I'm sorry about that bit, sir, very sorry. But you see, sir, I didn't know about Weavel stuff..."

"That is no excuse, Trainee!" said Captain Steadfast sternly. "It's for you to obey the rules and use the front door of the Academy..."

"Which I will do in future, sir, oh yes! No back doors for me in the future..."

"We will discuss your future another time, Tickle," said Lieutenant Duffle drily. "I think for now that we'd better stick to this incident. Do you understand what would have happened if you had simply allowed the pipe to do its proper work?"

"No, sir. Sorry, sir."

"The pipe was in place because it had been used to cleanse the room with the Water of Sound Doctrine. One of our Water of Sound Doctrine Keepers was manning it from the outside, and, once we were alerted to the incident, we were prepared to re-cleanse the room with Water of Sound Doctrine – which would have immediately melted the snow and killed the Weavel. We were preparing to release the water when you pressed the switch."

Gamrie was frankly astonished. "Really, sir? Well, well! Fancy that! I never thought of that, not once!"

"I think we realised that, Tickle," said Professor Stigmine.

"And to think that it sucked up all that snow instead!"

"The sucking action is usually used to collect Water of Sound Doctrine," observed Lieutenant Duffle.

The Professor scrutinised young Trainee Tickle – who seemed not so much upset about the incident as intrigued. "It seems that your friend, Trouble, is still dogging your footsteps, Tickle," she said.

But Trainee Tickle shook his head at that. "No, ma'am," he said emphatically. "He's really *not* my friend!"

Not much of any useful sense could be derived from further conversation with Gamrie, but you might be wondering what happened to all that snow…

What happened to the snow?

Imagine the sight of a massive pipe spewing vast quantities of snow out of a small window in the Academy, all the way into the street at the front of the gigantic fortress. Outside, Aletheians began to congregate – pointing and gesturing. A blizzard was blowing into the road – from a small window high up in the Academy! You could watch it, and touch the snowflakes, and even rush in and out of it – and yet remain in the sheltered calm of a quiet December day. It was a most peculiar experience.

Children rushed to the scene after school. The snow had stopped falling by then – but the scene that greeted them was still wonderful. The afternoon was turning frosty and borrowing freezing air from the night. Cascading from high in the Academy, over turrets and rooftops, all the way down the thick stone walls, into the street below, was a covering of deep glistening snow. It was the most spectacular sledging trail you could possibly imagine.

That night, the snow froze. Over the Christmas holidays the children were allowed to take their sledges and climb up the slope and whizz down the track into the road until the snow ran out.

Gamrie took his sister, Belle, sledging too.

It was the most unusual snowfall Aletheia had ever had for Christmas.

More about Nea Stigmine

I should add one final thing before this story is complete. Shortly after the events in this account, Professor Nea Stigmine married Dr Theo Pentone, who was at that time the Chief Scientist of Aletheia. Later they had a son – also called Theo Pentone. One day he would become the Director of Health and Chief Scientist at the Academy of Soldiers-of-the-Cross. To put it in a nutshell – one day he would do the jobs of both his clever parents combined. If you've read *The Mustardseeds* you'll know exactly who I mean, and he features in the following story too. You might also remember that in *The Rumour Mill*, Dr Theo Pentone's mother appears for a short time, when she's an old lady; but even then she's still one of the cleverest people in Aletheia.

LET IT SNOW!

Bible Verses

1 John 1:9:

'If we confess our sins, He is faithful and just to forgive us our sins and to cleanse us from all unrighteousness.'

1 John 3:2-3:

'Beloved, now we are children of God; and it has not yet been revealed what we shall be, but we know that when He is revealed, we shall be like Him, for we shall see Him as He is. And everyone who has this hope in Him purifies himself, just as He is pure.'

Bible Lesson – Be Clean!

1. In this story, Gamrie used a short cut (a back door) to get into the Control Room – and carried contamination where it shouldn't have been. In God's service, we must be careful that we don't carry contamination about with us. This can happen if we pick up wrong thoughts, or attitudes, or actions from people around us, instead of taking all we need from the Bible. We must be careful to be clean from contamination every day – by reading the Bible and praying.

2. Like the Weavel Seeds, small things can cause big problems if we allow them into our lives and don't keep clean.

3. And remember, contamination can spread to people around us and cause damage and destruction. What we do has an effect on other people too.

7. THE ESCAPE ARTIST

There are still plenty of stories to recount, but I think we've just got time for one more about Gamrie Tickle. This one takes place later in his training to be a Rescuer: in fact, when he's grown up and much older.

You see, Gamrie's training to be a Rescuer took far longer than most people's. He worked his way around all of the departments, but he didn't seem to fit any one speciality in particular; quite often he failed exams and tests. So he just kept training and working his way around all of the departments, even when he was an older man. Gamrie still holds the record for the longest time served as a Trainee Rescuer at the Academy. I don't think that record will ever be broken.

One night, Trainee Tickle was running late for his nightshift on guard in the dungeons of the Academy of Soldiers-of-the-Cross. This was no great surprise to anyone: Gamrie was often late.

A young Private, Bourne Faithful, had been given responsibility for the trainees who had shifts on guard in the dungeons. He was sitting at a small desk, scrutinising lists of current 'captives' and their various requirements. He was beginning to wonder why Trainee Tickle hadn't yet reported for duty and what excuse he would offer this time.

Bourne was much younger than Gamrie: in fact, he was young enough to be his son. But the scar across his face, coupled with his habitually sober expression, made him seem much the wiser of the two.

"I'm sorry I'm late, sir…" Out of breath, Trainee Tickle arrived for his shift.

"Tickle." Bourne scanned the dishevelled recruit.

"Yes, sir, sorry, sir, you see…"

Bourne hastily intervened. "Never mind about that now. You have work to do. Your duties tonight are simple but absolutely essential." Private Faithful had learned how seriously Trainee Tickle took any duty that was deemed important.

But Gamrie didn't look so much impressed as suddenly amused. His eyes crinkled with laughter in his scruffy, half-bearded face that was never quite free from whiskers no matter how hard he tried to meet the Academy's standards for neatness. "Another Meddler machine?" he guessed and laughed loudly, as if he had just cracked the best joke in the world.

The reference was to the time when Gamrie had spent an entire nightshift guarding a locked cell that contained a small machine – a miniature printing press. What he didn't know was that it had, after all, contained a small sample of the poisonous gas of the Meddlers.

Bourne didn't find the occasion as funny as Gamrie did. He knew how dangerous Meddlers could be. "Not a machine," he said, when Gamrie's laughter subsided. "You'll be guarding two Sloths tonight."

From Gamrie came another gust of laughter. "I'll sleep all night guarding them!" he chortled. Then, catching the look on the young Private's face, he hastily added, "But of course I won't, sir, of course I won't. I've been through my training on Sloths, oh yes. They won't get the better of me wearing my armour of God!"

Bourne remarked drily, "Well, you could always start by putting it on, Tickle. You ought to know by now that you always..."

"Come prepared to work wearing the full armour of God... yes, sir, but you see, sir, I was on my way when..."

"Enough," said Bourne firmly, interrupting what would undoubtedly be a long and colourful explanation. "Equip yourself with all your protective armour of God immediately and relieve Trainee PeaceBe at Cell 45. You will not approach or attempt to speak to the Sloths. Watch from a distance of no less than two metres."

Gamrie sighed. He enjoyed talking to any creatures who could converse, no matter how badly their speech was impaired and how inadequate their conversation. Sometimes he even tried his best jokes on them.

Cell 45

He reached Cell 45 without mishap. Small puffs of cloudy vapour shifted through the bars of the cell into the corridor, evidence of the Sloths within.

Gamrie greeted Trainee PeaceBe cheerfully. "Are you glad to see me?! Bet you slept through your whole shift guarding Sloths, eh?" He elbowed the unresponsive PeaceBe in the ribs. Then he stopped abruptly in surprise. He had never thought PeaceBe fragile: quite the opposite. But PeaceBe tottered unsteadily and gave a harsh, guttural hiss.

"You need to see a doctor!" exclaimed Gamrie in surprise. "You've got a sore throat brewing and no mistake. It's been an odd summer for sickness, not that I'm sick much myself. Did you happen to drink water from Err by mistake? I heard recently of an infection, waterborne they say… a visit to the waters of Sanctification will soon make you well. And…" He searched his mind for the right Bible verses to help the situation but came up empty. It was all rather curious. PeaceBe was wrapped up as if he had a dreadful cold; even his face was concealed.

A muddle of conflicting thoughts collided in Gamrie's mind. He should surely fetch PeaceBe some help! The poor man was in a bad condition and even now was swaying unsteadily and trying to wander farther down the corridor – quite the wrong way. But he had been told to guard the Sloths; Private Faithful had specifically said it was important. He kept a wary eye on the staggering PeaceBe and peeped into Cell 45. It was pretty cloudy all around, which was what you expected with Sloths, and the Sloth in the cell was doing what all such creatures do best: sleeping the kind of sound sleep that made you terribly, overwhelmingly sleepy just observing it. One, then two, orangey-brown, cloudy eyes opened and winked lazily at

Gamrie. Then slowly, slow-ly, so-oo sl-ow-ly, closed, bit by tiny bit... and Trainee Tickle felt his eyelids begin to fall sl-ow-ly s-h-ut...

He jerked his eyes open and pinched himself soundly, leaving an angry red mark on his arm. He *must not* fall asleep.

His armour of God! Things had happened so quickly that he hadn't had time to put it on. It was the basic rule of training. Rescuers couldn't do anything without their protective armour, and right now he desperately needed it to fight off the effect of the Sloth so that he could help PeaceBe.

PeaceBe! Where had he gone? And his plan for once again borrowing PeaceBe's armour to save time going to find his own was also falling apart. Still, it was likely to be quicker borrowing from PeaceBe than finding his own. He began to go rapidly down the corridor in the direction he had last seen PeaceBe.

What happened to PeaceBe?

When he reached Cell 145, Gamrie remembered that he was meant to be guarding Cell 45, and was a hundred too far down the row. How had things gone so quickly awry? In Cell 145 there were the component parts of a robot. Gamrie spent some time watching it. He could see one eye in the robot's head; it kept winking feebly. Gamrie chuckled with enjoyment at the curious sight. He wondered what the machine-cum-creature would look like put back together again. Why did the parts of a robot warrant a locked cell? It couldn't possibly get up and walk away. The dungeons were so very intriguing. He hoped he would be able to stay and work for young Private Faithful for a long time and explore the strange creatures and things that were locked away down here…

With a jolt, he once more remembered Private Faithful's instructions and his current duties at Cell 45. At least the Sloth was likely to be sound asleep. Could it possibly slip through the bars? It was made of… well, cloud, wasn't it? But then they wouldn't put it behind bars if it could get out, would they? Gamrie didn't always understand the decisions made by the hierarchy of the Rescuers, although he had great respect for their wisdom. The dilemma that now faced him was that there was no sign whatever of the departed PeaceBe, and meanwhile Cell 45 was left unguarded.

Gamrie sighed. Once more he wondered how things had gone wrong so quickly. With any luck he could rush back to Cell 45 and carry on as normal. He would have to be extra vigilant on guard without his armour, but he could get through the night and hopefully Private Faithful wouldn't know anything was amiss. It was an incredibly optimistic plan under the strange circumstances, and it fell apart as soon as Trainee Tickle, rushing headlong back up the corridor, spied the cluster of ranking Rescuers gathered around Cell 45.

There was nowhere for him to hide.

Private Faithful immediately spotted him approaching. Abruptly he said, "Tickle! Explain yourself!"

Gamrie's heart sank. He liked and respected the young

Private. Bourne Faithful was something of a star in the Rescuers; he was very young to have completed his training and be a Private, and Gamrie had certainly never intended to let him down. And then his heart sank even further as he recognised Captain Robert Steadfast, the leader of the Rescuers.

He tried to explain. "It was PeaceBe, sir. He was ill and… well, confused, I reckons, and he went that way." He pointed back down the gloomy corridor from whence he had lately come. "I was worried about him, you see, sirs, so I went after him…"

"Where is your armour, Trainee?" demanded Captain Steadfast sternly.

"Not on, sir," said Gamrie sadly.

"We'll deal with that matter later," said the captain abruptly. He nodded to Bourne to continue.

Bourne didn't waste words. "How exactly do you explain this, Tickle?" He pointed through the group of assembled Rescuers to a dazed and bloodied form being examined by a doctor in a white coat. The injured figure was sitting on the floor, wrapped in a blanket, leaning against the old stone wall of the fortress, making feeble attempts to stand…

Trainee Tickle gaped in astonishment.

The figure was PeaceBe!

Another enquiry

The incident in the dungeons was far too serious to leave

until the morning. Despite the fact that it was now night, an enquiry was hastily convened. At the head of a large table was Captain Steadfast, tall, stately, and no-nonsense. Many of the trainees had never met the captain, but Gamrie had been in such situations before, and, while he never felt at ease under the captain's stern scrutiny, he thought of this man as a great hero.

Private Bourne Faithful, as the officer on watch at the time of the incident, was sitting at the captain's right hand. A young man in a rumpled lab coat was next to Bourne. This was Dr Theo Pentone Jr., the recently appointed Director of Health and Chief Scientist at the Academy of Soldiers-of-the-Cross. Gamrie didn't know much about him except that he was already widely accepted to be the cleverest man in Aletheia. There was a young volunteer student, Harold Wallop, on work experience. He was taking notes at the enquiry, showing his keenness despite the late hour. In addition, there were a couple of other Rescuers who were ready to gather information or fetch and carry whatever might be required.

Gamrie did not actively dislike enquiries – truth be told, he secretly enjoyed the attention. But this was something different. Those gathered here were not so much interested in the details of his story or even his conduct – it seemed they had far more serious concerns.

Captain Steadfast was leading the questioning. "Describe the appearance of what you thought was Trainee PeaceBe."

"Ill, sir," said Gamrie earnestly. "Very ill. In fact, I remember telling him that he had picked up one of those waterborne sicknesses and that he might want to consider the waters of Sanctification..." He had hoped this might at least gain him an approving nod, but he was disappointed.

Captain Steadfast did not look impressed. He didn't seem to understand what Gamrie had meant at all. "Let's think about the detail," he interrupted. "What colour was his face?"

Trainee Tickle screwed up his features in earnest concentration. "His face? I'm thinking, sirs, I'm thinking," he said, in case this wasn't obvious. "His face, let me think about his face..."

Bourne gave an exasperated sigh. It was no use trying to hurry Gamrie Tickle – but *not* hurrying him was proving extremely trying.

"His face," Gamrie suddenly brightened. "Of course, he had no face!"

"No face...!"

"Well, of course he had a face," Gamrie tried not to get carried away with the sudden itch of amusement that plagued him as he fleetingly imagined what people would look like without faces. But even he realised a joke was not going to go down well at this juncture. "What I mean, sirs, is that it was all covered up, all muffled-like, so I couldn't see his face at all!"

Bourne could not resist muttering, "That didn't strike you as suspicious, I suppose...?"

From Dr Pentone, seated next to Bourne, there came what sounded like a chuckle.

"But I'm sure there was a face there, sirs, oh yes, I'm sure there *must* have been a face, under the muffles, sirs, hidden away. After all, you'd hardly expect PeaceBe to lose his face now, would you…?" His voice wavered with that sudden urge to laugh at the joke of PeaceBe without a face. Gamrie found it impossible to remember that the *thing* he saw was *not* PeaceBe at all.

Captain Steadfast interrupted, immediately quelling Gamrie's urge to laugh. "Why, then, did he strike you as *ill*?" They had been trying to elicit even the most basic details for some time already and the captain's voice was becoming strained. It was evident Trainee Tickle was trying to do the best he could, but it was clear that his memory was muddled by the sleep-inducing cloudiness of the Sloth that, without his armour, he could not withstand.

"He was…" Once more Trainee Tickle screwed up his face in concentration. "He was sort of staggering and making strange noises… not like PeaceBe at all!"

Bourne muttered, "Which is precisely what it wasn't."

This time Gamrie heard. "Well, no, of course not, sir," he said. "But you see, I didn't realise that at the time, didn't realise it at all…"

Bourne bit his lip to keep from further remarks. He was here to help in a difficult situation, not to vent his frustration on the exasperating Tickle.

"Didn't you think it odd that PeaceBe wasn't wearing his armour of God?" demanded Captain Steadfast.

"His armour of God!" exclaimed Tickle, realising this for the first time. "I knew there was something strange."

Once more, Bourne muttered, "That's the *only* strange thing you noticed about the situation?"

"His armour of God," continued Tickle, as if to himself. "I *knew* there was *something*. And to think I planned to use..." He trailed off, remembering just in time that his explanation that he had planned to borrow another trainee's armour was not going to help his chances to clear his name. Then another thought struck him. "Will I be allowed to continue to work for Private Faithful in the dungeons?" he enquired anxiously.

From Bourne there was a strange choking sound; from the others in the room a rustle of amusement; from the captain no sympathy at all. "We have yet to ascertain why you weren't adequately equipped with your armour of God for your shift, Trainee!" he said. "You were clearly not prepared to guard the two Sloths, or to detect that a dangerous intruder was loose in the Academy!"

Dangerous intruder! What was the captain talking about? But that matter oddly paled into insignificance when Gamrie contemplated that he might no longer be allowed to work for Private Faithful in the dungeons. He had undoubtedly let the Private down and, with that recollection, came a fresh concern.

"I'd like to say, sir," he said bravely, "that the young Private Faithful here told me to put on my armour. It's not his fault that I didn't get PeaceBe's armour in time..."

There was a short, stunned silence in which the student,

Harold Wallop, put down his pen and stared at the unhappy Tickle in astonishment.

"If I am to understand by that that you intended to borrow PeaceBe's armour of God for your own shift, that's a matter we will definitely consider at your appraisal," the captain said coldly.

Bourne was incredulous. "Did PeaceBe remove his armour to give it to you for your shift?"

Gamrie shrugged sheepishly. He really didn't want to land PeaceBe in trouble for removing his armour at the end of a shift to lend it to him. But it was what they had done before...

Captain Steadfast remarked, "This would certainly explain why PeaceBe was not prepared to defend himself..." He cleared his throat. "But right now, we would like the details of this incident in order to provide a remedy for the injured Trainee PeaceBe, and also so that we can discover whether the intruder we appear to have in the Academy poses an imminent danger to our city! Are we clear?"

Gamrie nodded glumly. Then, oddly, unusually, his face cleared as he suddenly recollected a detail he had not remembered before. "There might be something, Captain-sir," he said eagerly.

"Yes?"

"You said *two* Sloths!"

"Yes, the two Sloths in Cell 45..."

At last Gamrie felt useful, even important. He knew something that they didn't know. "Not two Sloths, sir! Just *one*!"

Discoveries

For the first time since entering the enquiry, Gamrie was pleased with the interest he had sparked. He wasn't sure why, but, to start with, they seemed inclined to doubt his word that there was only one Sloth. Private Faithful was adamant that there were two Sloths in Cell 45 when he did his rounds shortly before Tickle arrived for duty. But the young Dr Theo Pentone was very interested in his account of one Sloth and Gamrie was unwavering in his assertion that there were definitely only two orangey-brown eyes that winked and blinked at him and made him feel so sleepy. Dr Pentone kindly overlooked the part of the explanation about how Gamrie's eyes had closed. The young doctor focussed instead on rather odd details. Such as,

"Tell me, Tickle, did the creature you thought was PeaceBe speak with a hiss?"

Gamrie looked at the brilliant doctor in the stained lab coat that he had probably forgotten he was wearing. He seemed so ordinary and reassuring, unlike the captain in his smart uniform.

"A hiss! He wasn't a snake, sir, oh no! Even I might have recognised if PeaceBe had turned into a snake!" And Tickle allowed himself a chuckle for the first time since he had entered the daunting room and this serious enquiry.

But Dr Pentone didn't laugh. "I'm not interested in whether you thought he was a snake, Tickle," he said briskly. "From what you've described, all you could perceive was a shape covered in PeaceBe's clothes, shambling and stumbling and making strange noises..."

"That's it, sir!" interjected Gamrie in relief. At last someone had put into words exactly what he had seen.

"Think about the noises," urged the doctor. "Was there a hisssss, like thissss..." His remarkable intonation and accurate imitation of a snake was rather startling in the stillness of the room. Even the imperturbable captain turned curiously to Dr Pentone. And the effect on Gamrie was instantaneous.

For the first time he looked as if he knew what they were talking about. "Yes, sir! That's it, sir! A hiss!"

Dr Pentone was calm and unsurprised. "Very good. Now, think carefully again. Was there a smell?"

"A smell?" Trainee Tickle reverted to screwing up his face in intense concentration. "I don't think PeaceBe would smell, sir..."

"It *wasn't PeaceBe*! Do pay attention, Tickle!" cried the doctor. "Did the creature in the clothes, with the hiss... *did it smell*?"

Gamrie *did* pay attention. There was something in the man's urgency that compelled him to. "A smell," he said considering. He closed his eyes. Pictured that gloomy, half-lit corridor. It was dim. It was cool. Clean, of course. Everywhere in the fortress was clean. The stone-flagged corridor was smooth and footsteps echoed as you walked. Was there a smell down there in those brief moments outside Cell 45? *Was there a smell?*

At last he said slowly, "No smell, sir, that I can remember, sir. But there was something, sir…" Was it important? Suddenly he hoped so. He had no idea what they were so urgent and excited about or why they thought there was an intruder they should worry about. What was the big deal with a Sloth, and the strange, sort of maimed creature that had stumbled away down the corridor? He had forgotten the mysterious injury to PeaceBe and what this might mean.

"What is it?" urged the doctor. "Any details might help!"

For once, Trainee Tickle got straight to the point. "There were no footsteps, sir," he said simply. "No footsteps at all!"

The moments that followed Gamrie's revelation were always afterwards confused in his memory. His comment about no footsteps accompanying the stumbling figure that wasn't PeaceBe excited the youthful doctor a great deal. He asked more questions. About the way the creature walked. About how quickly it moved. About its hands, its feet – or shoes. Gamrie answered what he could and Dr Pentone dashed from the room to consult his books and the latest reports from the land of Err through the Central Control Room. "Could it be?" they heard Dr Pentone muttering to himself. "Have they advanced so far with the Deceivedors?"

Captain Steadfast, acting on a hurried consultation with the doctor, dispatched one of the Rescuers present at the meeting to the dungeons immediately. "Cell 45!" he barked out. "All Rescuers on standby to Cell 45. *Immediately!*"

The first Deceivedor

Gamrie didn't think it was quite right that he was excluded from the excitement that followed. When he later told the story you could have been forgiven for thinking that Trainee Gamrie Tickle was in the thick of the action that led to the discovery of the first Deceivedor. The truth of the matter was, however, somewhat different.

Under the unwavering supervision of Sergeant Troop, Gamrie worked the remainder of that memorable night in the massive armoury of the Academy – cleaning and tidying armour, so that he might never again forget how important it was.

Meanwhile, a Rescuer force, under the charge of Captain Steadfast himself, hemmed in Cell 45. Had Gamrie been present, it would have appealed to his own peculiar brand of humour that so many important, fully armed Rescuers gazed at two soundly sleeping, harmless Sloths. For there were *two* Sloths once more in Cell 45.

Slowly shifting cloudy vapour moved lazily around the cell and sometimes crept in small puffs between the bars. The only movement from the two Sloths was their deep breathing that would send any unprepared person deeply to sleep. But those gathered outside the cell were fully armed and equipped in their armour of God. The all-invasive sleepy-substance of the Sloths could not penetrate the helmet of salvation that a properly prepared Rescuer wore.

The group clustered at Cell 45 appeared to be waiting for something. At last there came the sound of hurrying footsteps, and the figure of Dr Pentone, also fully armed, came into view. He didn't waste time on pleasantries. He waved a large book in the air that he promptly handed to the nearest Rescuer.

Abruptly he said, "It's as I thought. Precisely what we could expect from the development of Deceivedors." He worked his way through the crowd of Rescuers to the captain at the front. "The Err folk at the Academy of Science-Explains-All *have* been busy! Reports from the Control Room concur. Imitating something like a Sloth would be an early advancement, so we can be thankful that they haven't yet developed the ability for Deceivedors to change into other creatures, or into human likeness. Sloths are about the easiest form to copy since their outline is so vague and all they do is, well... sleep! No clear speech involved, just shapeless movement..."

All the while he was talking, Dr Pentone was peering closely through the bars of Cell 45 at the two sleeping creatures.

Captain Steadfast asked quietly, "You think that Deceivedors imitating humans will develop in the future and threaten Aletheia?"

"Undoubtedly they'll try it at some point, but we now have an early type of Deceivedor placed into our hands to study and prepare against!" said the doctor. "We can learn a lot from this creature without the Academy of Science-Explains-All knowing the half. Now, can we have the cell opened please..." Dr Pentone removed his Bible from the pouch at his side and opened it. Rays of bright light shone around him.

"Private!" commanded Captain Steadfast.

Private Faithful immediately stepped forward and unlocked the cell door. All of the Rescuers present unsheathed weapons and stood ready to capture and defeat whatever creature was revealed within.

At first, nothing happened. The two cloudy Sloths continued to sleep soundly, their sides moving slowly up and down with deep, peaceful, unperturbed breathing.

The doctor moved cautiously, his Bible extended in his hand.

Then, as the radiant light from the Bible reached the sleeping pair, the most astonishing thing happened to one of the Sloths. The tranquil cloud-creature recoiled suddenly as if struck with something deadly. It rose high into the air above the youthful doctor, roiling and rolling like an angry storm cloud, turning darker and blacker, changing from cloud to substance, elongated, writhing, and at last deadly – as the form of an angry snake emerged, with evil red eyes and wicked, venomous fangs.

Captain Steadfast, a couple of his trusted lieutenants, and Private Faithful rushed quickly to Dr Pentone's side. The giant snake reared high above them, seeking to strike them with its sharp fangs. Again and again it recoiled and weaved, its head darting lightning fast, seeking a way through their defence. And again and again, with great skill and agility, the weapons of Captain Steadfast and his troops slashed at the snake. Until at last the snake toppled down.

It lay still in a pool of its own blood and venom, oozing and sticky and disgusting.

The snake was dead.

"A pity," said the doctor, as he bent over the body. "I would have liked it alive, but there's still plenty of material to examine here…" Ignoring the filth and stench of the liquid still leaking from gashes in the snake, oblivious to everyone else, he pulled glass vials, syringes, and various containers from his pockets and began taking samples. "I'll be able to ascertain the type of poison affecting Trainee PeaceBe," he said. "We'll have an antidote available in no time." Captain Steadfast quietly sent for members of the doctor's considerable staff of scientists and technicians to help.

Private Faithful, alert and watchful, guarded the doctor as he worked. He wondered if he would ever encounter anything like this again.

Clear up

Of course, there were further matters to clear up following the destruction of the Deceivedor. Trainee PeaceBe's clothes, 'borrowed' by the shape-shifting snake after it had overcome him, were found in a huddle in Cell 79. It was the only evidence of where the Deceivedor had been, and, perhaps, why. This cell contained… but that's a long story best left for another time. For our account it is enough to know that Cell 79 was as far as the creature went, turning back to Cell 45 while the bumbling

Trainee Tickle went all the way to Cell 145 and back. Trainee PeaceBe quickly recovered following the administration of Dr Pentone's remedy. The unaccountable blindness of Gamrie in not noticing the injured PeaceBe outside Cell 45 was explained by the effect of the Sloth and the distraction of the Deceivedor. It would never have happened had Trainee Tickle been wearing his armour of God.

Gamrie did not return to duty at the dungeons of the Academy until he had worked in the armoury for six months, learning, and re-learning about the importance of the armour of God. He never again attempted to borrow armour from anyone else. When he did return to the dungeons, another Private was in charge. It would be many years before he worked for Bourne Faithful again. But one day, some years after this story, he drove Lieutenant Bourne Faithful and Private Harold Wallop on a journey to the town of Broken. You can read all about that adventure in *The Broken Journey*.

Many years down the line from this story, Deceivedors were developed into near-human form, with drastic consequences for Aletheia. You can read about this in *The Defenders of Aletheia*. And in that story, Bourne Faithful, then a Lieutenant, certainly did encounter these creatures again.

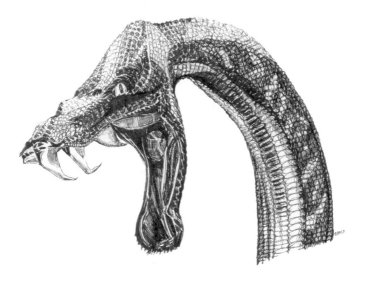

THE ESCAPE ARTIST

Bible Verses

1 Corinthians 1:9:

'God is faithful, by whom you were called into the fellowship of His Son, Jesus Christ our Lord.'

Psalm 31:23:

'The Lord preserves the faithful.'

Bible Lesson: Be Faithful!

1. In many ways, the lessons from this final story are similar to the first one – about being properly, personally prepared with our armour of God to work in God's service and do His will. Being consistent in Christian service, serving God every day, is what the Bible means by being faithful. God can protect, preserve and help those who are faithful to Him.

2. Once again, we need to remember that we must personally put on our armour of God at the beginning of every day – in order to be preserved in situations we will face, and serve God as we should.

3. Remember the way that the Deceivedor was unable to remain hidden or disguised once the light of the Bible shone on it? If we allow the Word of God to shine its light on something, we can judge it as it truly is. This means that we must test everything we're uncertain about by the principles and teaching of the Bible. Only then can we properly judge it as God sees it, and know whether it's right or wrong.

4. One more thing to note – it's a theme in all of these stories that Gamrie Tickle wasn't really fitted to work as a Rescuer the way he thought he was. He wanted the glamour and heroism and excitement of the work of a Rescuer – the way that plenty of Christians want a public, important role in Christian and church life today. But it is far more important to find the role for which God has fitted you, than seek one you might not be suited to. There is as much reward in a seemingly small, invisible work done for God, as there is in a public, exciting one.

A FINAL COMMENT

I hope you've enjoyed these stories about Gamrie Tiberius Tickle. If you want to read more about him, you can follow his daring adventure in *The Broken Journey*. In that story he's an old man who has at last discovered the work he's fitted to do for the Rescuers: he drives rescue vehicles on missions across the land of Err. But be on your guard! Remember that unexpected things generally happen wherever he goes...

I think they always will.

Did you spot all the characters from the Aletheia Adventure Series in the stories? Reuben Duffle, Dim View, Dismay Defeatia, Mrs De Voté, Dr Theo Pentone, Bourne Faithful, Harold Wallop... and there are family names which you might also remember – Straw, Steadfast, Steady, Wallop, PeaceBe – forebears of the great men and women who appear in subsequent adventures. If you don't already know about them and want to follow their stories, you can discover them in the Aletheia Adventure Series:

141

Book 1: The Rescue of Timmy Trial

Book 2: The Purple Storm

Book 3: The Broken Journey

Book 4: The Mustardseeds

Book 5: The Defenders of Aletheia

Book 6: The Rumour Mill

Bible Study Worksheets are available for this book. To download the worksheets, and for any other information, please visit:

www.aletheiabooks.co

ACKNOWLEDGEMENTS

Inspiration for this book:

In 2016, I heard from a young reader who had finished reading the six books in the Aletheia Adventure Series and had some excellent suggestions for future books. This included a request to hear more about Mr Tickle from *The Broken Journey* (Aletheia Adventure Series Book 3). I'm sorry it's taken so long, Patrick, but this is the book you asked for! I hope you enjoy it. I'm hoping to write more books in this series soon.

Thank you to readers:

A very big thank you to young readers whose feedback, ideas and encouragement I so appreciate. Patrick (whose idea sparked this book), Brice, Joshua, Emily, Toby, Ben, Luke, another Joshua, Rebekah, Michael, Stuart, and more. I love hearing from you!

Thank you to the book team:

Once again, I am greatly indebted to a group of people who have helped, advised and in so many ways supported the production of this book. In particular I would like to thank: Michael Wilkie, Ruth Hatt, Helen Munro, Anne Henderson, Sue Jackson, Ruth Chesney, and Margareta Lamacova. This book would simply not be possible without your help. A very big thank you to you all.